The Psychology of
Winning
for Women

What Every Woman
Needs to Know —

What Every Man
Needs to Understand

Denis Waitley, Ph.D.

Dayna Waitley, Ph.D., and Deborah Waitley, Ph.D.

Executive Excellence Publishing
1344 East 1120 South
Provo, UT 84606
phone: (801) 375-4060
fax: (801) 377-5960
web: http://www.eep.com

Ordering Information:
Individual Sales: Executive Excellence Publishing products are available through most bookstores. They can also be ordered direct from Executive Excellence at the address above.

Quantity sales: Executive Excellence Publishing products are available at special quantity discounts when purchased in bulk by corporations, associations, libraries, and others, or for college textbook/course adoptions. Please write to the address above or call Executive Excellence at 1-800-304-9782.

Orders for U.S. and Canadian trade bookstores and wholesalers: Executive Excellence Publishing books and audio tapes are available to the trade through LPC Group/Login Trade. Please contact LPC at 644 South Clark Street, Suite 2000; Chicago, IL 60605, or call 1-800-626-4330.

First edition

First printing 1999

Printed in the United States of America

10 9 8 7 6 5 4 3 2 1   04   03   02   01   00   99

ISBN: 1-890009-13-X

Cover design by Joe McGovern
Printed by Publishers Press

Endorsements

———●———

"The wisdom the Waitleys celebrates the gifts and strengths of women. Their time-tested winning tools are required for the 21st century Women. No matter what stage you are in on your journey, everyone can benefit from pausing and coming back to your own knowingness. This book helps you move ahead with clarity, commitment, strength, and joy!"
—Eileen M. Piersa, M.S.O.D., Vice President, Operations, Jenny Craig International

"A wonderful refresher on the principles of lifetime success, this book affirms how success is achieved, and it provides a 'rocket boost' of ideas, enthusiasm, and energy for taking initial success to new heights by turning 'stress' into 'stretch!'"
—Rebecca Campbell, SPHR, FLMI, Senior Vice President, Organization Development and Change Management, American General Life

"This book offers invaluable lessons from women who reach their initial goals and still strive further to achieve ultimate success. What an incredibly motivational tool!"
—Edie Lutz, Editor-in-Chief, *Women* Magazine

"A must-have for any woman who truly wants to succeed in business and leisure."
—Marchel Alverson, Editor, *Women in Business* Magazine

Dedication

———●———

This book is dedicated to women in every culture for whom winning is simply expressing their views and dreams without fear.

Acknowledgements

————————●————————

The authors would like to acknowledge the dedication and research of our colleague, Antonia Boyle, who turned a concept into substance.

We appreciate the confidence and vision of Ken Shelton, president of Executive Excellence Publishing, in affording us the opportunity to turn our ideas into a work that can benefit women and men throughout the world.

We thank each member of our family for contributing to the richness of our live, knowing that any of them could have written this book, equally as well, from a different perspective.

Contents

————————●————————

Foreword

---•---

by Susan Waitley

Being a wife, mother and, only recently, a career woman, I have a special feeling for the significance of this book, *The Psychology of Winning for Women*.

When I met Denis Waitley, I was a single mother with two grammar school-age daughters. While Denis and I were dating and wondering if we were soulmates "the second time around," he was laboring over the manuscript for his classic work, *The Psychology of Winning*.

I encouraged Denis to pursue his dream and maintain the belief and persistence that his creativity was worth being published and enjoyed by thousands of individuals.

We were married in the Spring of 1978, and later that year, Nightingale-Conant released his six-cassette audio album and, a few months later, the book that he had researched and nurtured during the previous 10 years. We both knew it had potential, but neither of us imagined that it was destined to become the all-time, best-selling program on personal excellence.

For more than 20 years, I have been a homemaker, wife, and mother for our combined family of six children. We also brought a girl from Mexico into our home, and she, as far as we're concerned, has become our fifth daughter, along with our two sons.

As Denis has traveled throughout the world lecturing to corporate, university, professional, sports, and public audiences, I have been pulled in two, diametrically opposite directions: the desire to share his experiences firsthand, and the desire to be a role model and mother at home with our children.

Although I managed to travel internationally with my husband, on occasion, I elected to devote the majority of my time and efforts to raising our family. Having lived through the experience of wanting to be two places at the same time and be two people at the same time, I understand the dilemma that women face throughout their lives in terms of duty versus desire. I have no regrets in the choices I made. In fact, I have discovered that there is a time for all things, and that roles change as do the seasons.

Denis and I are proud of our eldest daughters, Deborah and Dayna, who worked with their father to create this book. We are equally proud of our other children, each making a unique contribution in his or her own right: Denis Jr. for his athletic accomplishments and outgoing personality, Darren for his dedication to his family and service to others, Kimberlyn for her creativity and special child development skills, Lisa for mastering English and Chinese studies and becoming a fine English teacher and wife, and Graciela for her example as a gracious mother and caregiver.

Now that our children have grown and flown, building families and destinies of their own, I have discovered that it's never too late to chase your passion and explore your own potential. After 30 years in a supporting role, with no previous business experience, I am now the CEO of my own health products business, traveling globally.

Now my husband, Denis, faces those decisions that I faced earlier in our marriage. Should he focus on his commitments at home or join me in my adventures? I think he is as supportive of my search for self-actualization as I have been of his through the years.

What a time to be alive and be a woman! If a 50-something-year-old grandmother can launch a successful career, while still enjoying her relationship with her husband, children, and grandchildren, think of what you can do!

Enjoy the wisdom in this book, and then live your life, out loud!

Preface

———————•———————

What works for men isn't always as effective for women. Women bring special talents, skills and strengths to living and, by the same token, have special needs. Women speak in different metaphors, see with different intuitions, hear in different contexts, and feel with different emotional barometers. Women's lives are usually more complex because women usually have the responsibility for home and children, in addition to—not instead of—the challenges and callings of careers.

For these reasons, Denis, Dayna, and Deborah Waitley decided to have the principles of *The Psychology of Winning* reinvented to the particular needs of women. This book is a combination of time-tested ideas and new breakthroughs in behavioral research brought into the 21st century for women who seek to realize their full potential and become all they are capable of becoming in their personal lives, as well as their professional careers.

The name Denis Waitley is synonymous with the best in high level performance and personal development. In 1978, his landmark program, *The Psychology of Winning*, was first introduced in audio tape format. Since then, it has sold nearly two million copies, been published in book form, translated into many foreign languages, and used as a basic training tool by individuals and organizations worldwide from Olympic and professional athletes to corporate executives, government officials, educators, returning prisoners of war, families, and students of all ages. That program, and others he has researched and developed during the past 20 years, have become standards by which other personal and professional self-management programs are measured.

11

Psychology of Winning for Women

———————•———————

In *The Psychology of Winning*, Denis Waitley identified 10 qualities of a total winner—10 positive attributes and actions that are demonstrated by those high performance people who seem to get what they want in life in a very natural, free-flowing way. With them, he gave us the 10 keys winners use to unlock the door to authentic, lasting success.

A graduate of the United States Naval Academy at Annapolis and a former naval aviator, he has counseled Olympic athletes, Apollo Moon program astronauts, top sales and management executives and leaders in every field. He served as president of the International Society for Advanced Education, founded by Dr. Jonas Salk, and as Chairman of Psychology on the U. S. Olympic Committee's Sports Medicine Council, dedicated to the performance enhancement of all of the U. S. Olympic teams. He is one of the most sought-after keynote speakers and lecturers in the nation on self-leadership and the management of change.

In addition to being successful professionally, Denis Waitley has been successful personally. He and his wife Susan have raised six children, including four daughters who have achieved academic excellence, with masters or doctorate degrees, and careers spanning the spectrum from education to entrepreneur, from behavioral science to corporate consultant and platform speaker. Their father walked his talk, and his daughters consistently put into practice the winner's qualities they listened to repeatedly while growing up. More than hearing them, they also observed and experienced them in action daily. They know what their father teaches works effectively in the real world. At the same time, they realized that the world has changed since he conducted his major research effort. So Dayna and Deborah joined their father in recreating the classic *Psychology of Winning* just for women.

Introduction

———•———

by Denis Waitley

Years ago, when I first wrote *The Psychology of Winning*, I didn't give much thought to whether it would be read and used as a self-improvement program by men or women. I simply assumed that it would work for everyone. After all, I included many examples of women who had used the 10 qualities of a total winner to succeed. My mother and grandmother brought me up to think of women as equal—if not superior, in many respects—to men. And if I ever slipped back into male chauvinism, I had my wife and daughters to bring me quickly back to reality.

As our four daughters grew up in a world filled with male and female stereotypes, I watched their struggles within the system and realized that there is a difference between the genders. It shows up in the way they function in business, in their community, and at home in their personal relationships. The 10 qualities of a total winner are as valid today as they were when I first identified them, but my daughters changed and refined them through the years to make them more personal and pertinent for women.

I knew we needed another research project that presented the basic core values I had included in the original—synthesized, adapted, and reengineered, as well as augmented by the observations, wisdom and information gathered by women who had, as we say today, "been there, done that." What was needed was fresh, new material, presented for the 21st century woman.

13

Time and again, my daughters and I discussed what needed to be included as part of this new approach, until finally I threw the problem back into their laps. Dayna and Deborah, who had gone on to pursue their doctorate degrees in psychology, agreed to tackle the project—and that's how *The Psychology of Winning for Women* came to be.

Each of them is a prime example of today's active, multi-faceted, involved woman. They're uniquely qualified to share with you the qualities that combine to make every winner unbeatable. Not only have they been raised with *The Psychology of Winning*, they teach it and they live it, each in her own way. And that's what we hope this book will do for you. We want you to take the basic qualities and twist them, turn them, and reshape them until they fit you and your special circumstances. We want them to make a discernible change in your life.

Through our own trials and tribulations, sort of a real-life "Brady Bunch," we believe you will identify with the practical action steps in the chapters that go along with the core values we have identified. My wife, Susan, has been an inspiring role model for me and our children, and I give her a great deal of credit for being the glue that has held our family together through the years.

Chapter 1

●

Women Who Win

What you're about to read can change your life. How many times have you been promised that? Probably a lot. But in this case you're going to be pleasantly surprised, because this information will change the way you think—about yourself, your life, your relationships, your goals, your family—about everything that touches your life. We'll be giving you facts and figures, the latest information on studies and techniques, along with illustrations and real-life case histories to think about and learn from.

We'll also guide you as you reach down inside yourself to find answers to questions you may never have asked before. We hope they'll kick-start you into overdrive, just as they did us.

All our lives, we were told that there was nothing beyond our capabilities. We believed it. We want you to believe it, too. As the old ad campaign said, "You've come a long way, baby!"—and we've only just begun.

One of the important things we want you to realize is that this isn't just a "how to succeed in business for women" book. We'll certainly discuss women in the workplace, because over 75 percent of us are employed outside the home. But we'll also talk about women in many other aspects of our lives.

Vive la Différence!

We are complex creations. John Gray, who wrote *Men Are From Mars, Women Are From Venus*, pointed out that we think differently from men. Deborah Tannen, in her book, *You Just Don't Understand*, showed how we use the language differently. Men and women express emotions differently. We use our brains differently. Our dreams and goals may be parallel but not identical.

We approach tasks from different perspectives. Our metaphors are different. We're not as driven to "win at all costs" as most men are. We relate more to the common good than the individual triumph.

The former prime minister of Israel, Golda Meir, described some of the thought processes women go through. She said, "At work, you think of the children you have left at home. At home, you think of the work you've left unfinished. Such a struggle is unleashed within yourself. Your heart is rent." She's right. Many of us are torn apart trying to decide whether to stay home and nurture our children, or go out to work and help feed and clothe them, as well as develop our own potential. Many men don't feel this same ambivalence.

While business and sports are important to many of us, we aren't always as comfortable as men with the images, symbols, idioms, and anecdotes that seem to be the hallmark of many self-advancement programs.

● ● ●

Dayna Waitley: As a wife, mother and motivational speaker, I have tremendous admiration and empathy for the working mother. I continue to struggle and juggle my way through the balancing act of managing career and family.

I can remember the added tension I felt whenever my infant son, Alex, accompanied me to my out-of-state speaking engagements. I assembled diapers, bottles, and a bag of tricks for his entertainment needs. Despite the additional pressure, I still preferred the stress of traveling with him to the stress of being away from him.

I'll never forget a plane trip we took to Miami during his first year of life. Alex was sitting on my lap babbling, cooing, and making all sorts of loud vocalizations. I was concerned about him disrupting the other passengers, and I was frantically trying to keep him as quiet as possible. An elderly man from across the aisle leaned over and said, "You know, I think your son has political aspirations." I gave him a perplexed look and asked, "Why do you say that?" He winked and replied, "Because he sounds really good, but he isn't saying anything!"

As I smiled and laughed, my stress evaporated. I've since learned to keep my sense of humor about the inherent friction between my roles as an involved and dedicated parent, a support system for my husband, and as a professional motivator, lecturer, and author.

P.S. Many of you men go through the same struggles and conflicts between work and family, although perhaps not as pronounced as many women, or maybe not communicated as much. Let's work together to give each other strokes of empathy and compassion in our quest for balance and fulfillment in our lives.

• • •

We could devote this entire book to listing our differences, but we'd rather explore how to make those differences work for us—instead of against us. Our approach incorporates 10 positive qualities of a total winner and applies them specifically to women. We'll introduce many of today's "winning" women. What obstacles did they overcome to achieve their best? What character traits do they have in common that make them so uncommonly successful?

How did they make a worthwhile contribution to their family, business, community, or planet? We'll ask what it takes to "win" as a woman. And how do we go about preparing, training, and coaching ourselves and others to win—and continue to win? We'll also ask: What do we have to do differently to get to the same place as our male counterparts and coexist? These are some of the questions we'll address.

Winning Redefined

Before we do anything else, we ought to define what we mean by "winning." We aren't talking about winning so that others lose. Instead, we're talking about winning so that we don't lose. And winning by helping others win.

This kind of winning has nothing to do with races or contests. At the summer Olympics in Atlanta, a highly criticized billboard and television commercial had this admonition: "You don't win silver. You lose gold." That sentiment is 180 degrees away from how we feel. You not only win silver, you win just because you competed.

We're talking about living your life successfully, based on what you want to achieve—being *your* best instead of being *the* best. It's your own personal pursuit of individual excellence. You don't have to get lucky or knock down other people or profit at someone else's expense. In our vocabulary, "winning" means taking the talent and potential you were born with, developing it, and focusing it fully in the direction of a goal or purpose that will make you happy.

• • •

Denis Waitley: I served as Chairman of Psychology on the U. S. Olympic Committee's Sports Medicine Council during the past decade, and I observed firsthand that at the world-class level, talent is nearly equal. In competition, the mental conditioning is just as important as physical conditioning. Attitude is the winner's edge. It is the lock on, or key to, your door of success. That's why this book will concentrate on the mindset of high-performance, healthy human beings, not stories of super-achievers.

We'll talk about the stories of athletes who achieve through physical performance. But you'll understand that physical performance by the human body is accomplished by following directions sent by the mind as a result of mental practice and focused thinking. When the mind speaks, the body listens and acts accordingly!

All great athletes stand in the winner's circle only after they have visualized their success over and over in their minds. A tremendous amount of athletic training takes place in the brain.

The psychology of winning we're talking about is the sum of traits, attitudes, thoughts, and actions of an achiever—someone who's fulfilling her potential. Most of the successful people we write about are women. Some of them will be very familiar to you. Others may not be as well known. But each will have accomplished something that makes her stand above the crowd. We'll identify the traits, attitudes, thoughts and actions necessary to be successful and fulfilled as a woman today.

• • •

The Glass Ceiling Isn't Glass

For centuries women have been perceived to be the "lesser" and "weaker" gender. We've virtually always been placed in a supporting role that shows us winning silver or bronze, while the superior man takes the gold. We have been brought up to honor, serve, support, and defer to men. Even the history books put women in the background. Until recently, women's contributions were more of a curiosity than a matter of any significance. Their roles were largely ignored.

Here's a trivial but telling example. Many of us have delivered a baby by Cesarean section. Did you know the procedure is named after the Roman emperor, Julius Caesar? Legend has it he was the first person delivered in that manner.

You'll notice, however, the procedure isn't named after his mother. Her identity seems lost in antiquity—even though she, we presume, did all the work—and undoubtedly died in the process. Men wrote the history books.

Women have been rallying for equal rights for many years. However, our societal conditioning seems to pull us up short just when we begin to get a little ahead of the game. That's why this book is geared specifically to you—a woman facing the brightest future imaginable, with a new century at your feet and the experiences of generations who have gone before to learn from. The proof of the advances we've made—and those we haven't made—is found in the statistics. It's amazing how far women have come on the one hand, and how far we have to go on the other. Let's take a quick look at some facts and figures.

In 1970, law degrees were conferred on 1,240 women, compared to 16,181 men; 20 years later, American law schools graduated 16,302 women compared to 21,643 men. And the number of women in law schools today is still increasing, compared to men. Yet, ironically, in some countries, women cannot testify in a court of law or serve on the bench as judges.

Graduates in all branches of medicine have risen just as fast. The number of women in medical and dental schools has risen dramatically, as has the number of women pursuing engineering degrees. Women are definitely being represented in the sciences. However, only 3 percent of the members of the National Academy of Science are female. It proves we may earn the degrees, but the acceptance by our male peers comes more slowly.

And in business, 5 percent of 1972 MBA graduates were women, compared to over 40 percent today. As we travel throughout the country talking to the deans of business schools in major colleges and universities, they tell us that there are about as many women currently enrolled in graduate business programs as there are men.

This causes us to ask ourselves: Does the glass ceiling still exist now that there are many more executive women in the work force? The answer is: You bet it does! But we're discovering more and more about the ceiling, particularly how to get around it and break through it.

Anne Jardin, cofounder of the Simmons Graduate School of Management, said, "We don't accept the 'glass ceiling' notion here. The ceiling isn't glass; it's a very dense layer of men."

Perhaps that explains why in the five years between 1982 and 1987, the number of businesses owned by women grew 57 percent. By 1999, 5 million businesses were owned and managed by women. Many of them had decided that if you can't break through the glass ceiling, move to a new building where there are no ceilings. I think here we have to admit that while women have been stepping into "traditionally male roles," we have also been stepping on "traditional male toes."

The woman who's equally educated, equally competent, and equally ready to do the job is often perceived not so much as a colleague as a threat. She threatens a man's security, his masculinity, and his preconceived notions of the world order. His natural response is to squash the intruder. Her equally natural reaction is to preserve her gains. And so the battle escalates.

A recent poll of American women found that nearly 90 percent feel that men's attitudes need to change before equal rights can be achieved in the home and at work.

Women and Men: Equal Partners

We want to get something straight right away. This book isn't designed to complain about men. There's been too much of that since the Women's Liberation Movement started in the 1960s. We have no ax to grind with men. Our father has been a warm, loving, positive force in our lives. We're close to our significant male partners, our male family members, our male friends, our male coworkers, and other male role models. It's important that women appreciate what men bring to our lives.

We are like the two sides of a piece of Velcro—apart, neither side performs as well as it's meant to. Put the sides together and they form a strong bond that enables them to function superbly. We need to remember that the two sides of a piece of Velcro are equal. Although they're different in make-up and looks, no one side is considered superior to the other. Each has a specific purpose. No one side is more important than the other to the functioning of the whole. No side can do the job completely alone. Instead, to work well, they must combine their individual abilities and mesh evenly.

It's been said that if we don't pay attention to history, we are doomed to repeat it. Let's not let that happen. Instead of replaying history (or pronounced another way, His-Story) let's write Her-Story instead—and *The Psychology of Winning for Women* is just the beginning. We're going to take you on a journey to explore your past, present, and options for the future. We want you to be enlightened, inspired, and fulfilled. And we want you to always remember, we're just showing you how to plan the route and draw the map. The journey is up to you!

Your Personal Journal

We'd like to make one more suggestion as we begin. In the chapters that follow, we ask a number of questions. Some of these require you to write a sentence, paragraph, or more, and all of them take reflection and introspection. There'll be lists, promises, and decisions to make. We also raise a number of issues about which you may have strong opinions. And you will be turning dreams into goals, goals into commitments, and commitments into plans and action steps.

We suggest that you keep a journal close at hand. A journal is different from a diary. A diary is a chronicle of what has happened in your life. A journal is a preview of coming attractions and what you intend to make happen. If you don't have one—attractive, inexpensive books of blank paper are readily available in every bookstore, office supply and variety store.*

You also might want to buy a pen that writes in a different color of ink than you've ever used before. Some people like to keep their journals in purple ink, or turquoise, or whatever color makes them react positively.

Make this journal as personal and meaningful as you possibly can. It will become your friend and confidante—and no one else ever has to see it if you don't want them to. Whatever you do, make the journal meaningful to you.

As we go along, answer the questions in your journal. Write notes to yourself. Paste in pictures that remind you of things you want in life. Jot down quotations that you read or hear which have particular meaning for you. Write out your fears—you'll find they're less concerning when you see them on paper. Keep a record of your triumphs, no matter how

*We are creating a Psychology of Winning journal to complement this book. To order, call 1-800-304-9782.

small you think they are. And don't worry about how well you write or what your handwriting looks like. No one else is going to see this but you. Your journal will become a good friend. Don't put it off. Start working on it today.

• • •

Deborah Waitley: I was a teenager when I first began keeping a diary, the chronicle of my tireless flirtations and frivolous escapades. It provided an outlet for the diffused energy state I was going through at the time. At age 26 I started a journal, and for the last 16 years it has been my constant companion and intimate confidante. Serving as a womb for my dreams, a sponge for my fears, and a vault for my secrets, journal writing has been one of the most powerful tools of transformation in my life. It can be whatever you make it: a record of your daily activities, a diatribe of injustices and negative occurrences, or a glorious treasure map in which you log your personal discoveries and insights along the terrain of life. It is often an exciting yet treacherous exploration of who you are. It will reveal a self you think you know, a self you don't yet know, and a self you always knew but have forgotten.

I believe everyone has a story to tell and that each life contributes in some way toward the common good. Keeping a journal challenges me to reflect on my experiences and extract the essence and meaning out of my ordinary existence—making my life quite extraordinary.

I consider the 61 journals I have written so far to be my most valuable possessions. Each time I begin a new journal I enter an uncharted phase of my life and am filled with the anticipation and excitement of creating something new on a blank page. This is how I view each day: a blank canvas to create an original work of art through the very act of living my life. I encourage each and every one of you to take this journey. Even if you don't like to write or don't feel you are a good writer, you can jot down ideas, add pictures and photographs, drawings and sketches, or paste in e-mails and insights. I guarantee that you will learn to accept and affirm yourself more fully as a result. And isn't that what winning is all about?

P.S. In case any of you male readers are dismissing journal writing as one of those "female things," check out the work of Leonardo Da Vinci, Carl Jung, and Walt Whitman—three avid journal writers. Some of the greatest discoveries, insights, breakthroughs, and contributions to humankind began as journal musings.

• • •

Denis Waitley: Remember, what happened yesterday is history. Learn from it, but don't live there anymore. Tomorrow is a mystery. Don't be apprehensive about the future. View it with eager anticipation. Today is a gift to delight in the minute it is opened. That's why today is called "The Present." Your *Psychology of Winning for Women* begins in this present moment.

In the next chapter, we'll be talking about the primary need each woman has—the need to be aware and accept that she has more inner potential to discover than she could ever use in a thousand years.

What Every Woman Needs to Know

- You don't need to "beat someone" to win. Winning is setting high internal standards and living up to them.
- The glass ceiling is real and present. But it isn't glass at all—it's a very dense layer of men. Be prepared to put in more effort and contribution to gain parity with men.

- You don't need to behave like a man to succeed in the new millennium. As you'll discover throughout this book, the profile of the global leader in the 21st century favors women's natural and developed traits.
- The goal is not to become antagonistic to men, but to become synergistic.
- "Winning at all costs" has been a male motto. In a borderless world, team building and strategic alliances are critical to surviving and thriving. Instead of the "everyone's a competitor" mentality, a more effective mindset is "everyone's a customer."

What Every Man Needs to Understand

Competition—be it in the marketplace, polling place, or playing place—sharpens skills, exposes inferior efforts, stands guard against greed, and motivates us to be the best we can be.

But what is still missing in today's male-oriented society is a spirit of cooperation, team synergy, and creativity—a feeling that it is more important to help everyone develop his or her potential as a human being rather than to simply get on the scoreboard and add another win to the victory column.

In a world grown smaller as a result of instant access to information, strategic alliances, and allegiance to trusted brands and relationships, it is vital for men to understand that cooperation dosen't need to mean compromising values. Listening for common needs and goals is a strength that needs to be developed in the 21st century leader.

Now and in the future, "If you go for the jugular, you will cut your own throat!"

Chapter 2

———•———

Discover Your Potential

*I*n this chapter, we talk about the first characteristic of the achiever—self-acceptance. Women who win in life accept themselves as they are: changing, growing, imperfect, and in the process of becoming all their potential allows them to be. Self-acceptance means being open to possibilities and expanding horizons. When we know who we are, we know we have an abundance of talent and inner resources to tap. We know we have acres of uncut diamonds in our minds.

The first characteristic of a winning woman today is the attitudinal quality of self-acceptance—viewing yourself as a work of art in progress over an entire lifetime.

Winners know who they are, what they believe, the role in life they are currently filling, their own unlimited personal potential—and they have future plans and goals which will take them to the fulfillment of that potential. Winners are honest with themselves and others. Self-acceptance is their moment of truth.

This is very important. "Self-acceptance is the moment of truth." In this chapter, we talk about truth—about being able to look at yourself as the person you were, the person you are, and the person you can be. We want you to look at yourself honestly, without pride or modesty.

This will allow you to understand the ways in which you are unique—the gifts you have been given and the even greater gifts you have to give. As Doris Mortman wrote: "Until you make peace with who you are, you'll never be content with what you have."

Burning the Bridges of Stereotype

If you're like a lot of women, you've been selling yourself short most of your life. You've been conditioned to believe that true womanhood is exemplified by "the dutiful daughter," "the accommodating wife," "the sacrificing mother," and "the over-worked employee." You were raised with images of women sacrificing themselves for their families.

Even the popular novel, *Bridges of Madison County*, depicts the woman who sacrifices what she wants to serve her family. Now, we don't suggest that any woman should discard the life she has and run away with a roving photographer she just met. We do suggest, however, that this novel was written by a man who, once again, created the male version of an ideal woman.

She's warm, loving, sensual, cooks well, demands nothing for herself, and gives and gives without complaint. To hear the author, Robert James Waller, tell it, the essence of womanhood would seem to be unending service and silent endurance.

Don't misunderstand us. In no way do we disparage people—of either gender—willing to sacrifice for those around them. At the same time, we can't condone the martyr. The early feminist writer, Simone De Beauvoir, said that women are willing to be submissive "to avoid the strain involved in undertaking an authentic existence."

She thought that, as women, we found it easier to allow others to plan our lives and rule our worlds than to venture into the unknown and carve out our own paths.

Moving from Victim to Victorious

Admittedly, the role of the victim can become familiar and comfortable, making it harder to break out. Let's shout it, loud and clear—there are enough victims in this world!

There's no room for self-made victims in our world today. The popular radio personality, Dr. Laura Schlessinger, becomes angry with callers who suggest they're victims of someone else's behavior. She is on a campaign to wipe out the "poor-helpless-me" approach. She wants women to stand on their own two feet and demand the best for themselves. As she says, "What sells these days to women is the message, 'you're not to blame.' I'm telling women, 'Stop blaming men or society or anything else for your personal disappointments.'"

To feel worthy of success, to expect that the world gives us what we want, we have to believe we have the potential within us to succeed. Despite the enormous strides women have made since the 1960's, many of us still harbor some of what Colette Dowling called "The Cinderella Complex." No matter how much we achieve, no matter how large our paychecks, no matter how many honors are conferred upon us, we continue secretly to wait for the coach to turn back into a pumpkin, the horses once again to become mice, and to find ourselves, the morning after the ball, sweeping the ashes, wistfully hoping things will get better.

During the depression, a housewife with debilitating arthritis had to go out and earn her living. Lacking confidence and training, she took the only job she felt qualified for: selling household products door-to-door. She was good at it—so good, in fact, that in a very short time she became an area manager and had several people working for her.

But as her sales rose, she did not. She was held back because she was a woman. So in the early 1960s, she borrowed money, opened a store, and struck out on her own, promising herself that her company would be based on treating people with equal respect and offering women unlimited opprtunities.

This attitude has paid off *beautifully* for Mary Kay Ash and for the quarter of a million "Beauty Consultants" who sell Mary Kay Cosmetics directly to customers all over the world.

Mary Kay would tell you that her secret of successs has been to bring out the inner values in each person on her team and the Mary Kay attitude that there are no "lower" people. Everybody is treated the same. Corporate managers even spend a day each year in the factory so they can experience firsthand what it's like to work on the line.

She also would talk about the uphill transformation that has to take place in some of her new sales representatives. She said, "So many people just don't know how great they really are. They come to us all vogue on the outside and vague on the inside."

What a great description. A terrific looking package with very little inside. If you could see behind many elegant, well-groomed exteriors—behind many executive job titles—you'd find a little girl sitting in the cinders, waiting for the prince to come and save her because she doesn't feel she can do it on her own. If he doesn't come, she's not surprised. It meets her expectations.

It sounds simple enough to reverse this attitude. Just explore your potential and talents, and give yourself permission to pursue an exciting and fulfilling life. Of course, that's easier said than done. However, if you are one of the millions of women who isn't getting everything she wants—and deserves—from life, it's time for you to reverse your mindset. This means developing a finely tuned sense of self—of who we are and what we're doing here. Emily Hancock put it this way: "Many women today feel a sadness we cannot name. Though we accomplish much of what we set out to do, we sense that something is missing in our lives and—fruitlessly—search "out there" for the answers. What's often wrong is that we are disconnected from an authentic sense of self."

In her book *Something More: Excavating Your Authentic Self*, Sarah Ban Breathnach describes the journey toward authenticity as unveiling the mystery of our lives by digging deep to find our unfulfilled longings and abandoned dreams.

• • •

Deborah: It has taken many years to find my authentic self and move out from under a victim consciousness to a life most victorious. Discovering my potential was perhaps one of my greatest victories. People I meet almost always assume that because I am the daughter of Denis Waitley, a world-renowned author and motivational speaker recognized as an influential role model for success, that I have lived a charmed life.

They presume that I was somehow born into instant success with an easy and privileged life. Not true. We struggled like any other family trying to make ends meet. My greatest challenge as the daughter of such a successful and dynamic father has been finding my own identity and discovering my own unique potential within.

Maureen Murdock, author of the *Heroine's Journey* and the *Hero's Daughter,* talks about how many women have become separated from their feminine natures and have over-identified with the energy of the father. This split is reinforced in the world when we come into contact with society's patriarchal and masculine values. Having always sought my father's approval as a child, when the time came to move out on my own, I found myself still seeking constant validation from the external world—the man's world. I had lost my sense of self, my personal power.

For almost half my life, I have searched the world over for my true self. I finally realized what was missing was self-acceptance and self-love. I was forced to look deep within the hidden parts of myself to uncover my true nature and dormant potential.

I now accept myself as I am—as a woman. I don't have to be like a man, I don't need to prove anything to anyone,

I don't need to be successful in the same way as my father. I simply must be my own person, the one behind the mirror.

P.S. Many of you men also feel the pressures of living up to society's patriarchal standards and masculine values of success and achievement. Men, like women, become cut off from their feminine sides and can be ridiculed or made to feel "weak" if they display such qualities as sensitivity, an interest in fashion and design, or a disinterest in sports. The bottom line is to do what you can to discover your true potential, accept yourself for who you are, and "win" in those ways that are important to you.

• • •

Looking Behind the Mirror

That sense of self allows us to believe that we can be successful—and not just in business. To be a winner means being successful in several arenas, including your personal life, your relationships, your community, your education, your leisure times. It means caring for yourself physically, mentally, emotionally, and spiritually.

If you want to find out if you're winning in these arenas, think about your daily activities. Step back from your routine and assess what you are doing versus what you really want to do and can be doing. Here's a place you might want to make some notes in your journal.

When did you last stop to watch the sunset, or get up early to greet the dawn? How often do you turn off the television to talk to your inner circle, especially your children (if you have children and they are still at home), and share with them or read them a good book, or read one for yourself? Are you continuing to learn, even though your school years are long past? Have you donated any time or money to your favorite charity recently? Are you worried about money, or are you handling your finances wisely? Are you scheduling time for rest or relaxation, writing these appointments with yourself in your day planner? Do you plan time for exercise and then do it? Are you eating healthy foods to take care of your body? Are you aware of the latest scientific research on nutritional supplements, such as antioxidants, as it relates to degenerative disease and aging?

Current statistics say that the average woman can expect to live to be 82 years old. What are you doing to preserve your magnificent body machine so you will be healthy and alert every moment you're on this earth?

Age Is in the Eye of the Beholder

At a recent convention to select the presidential candidate for the national elections, one of the delegates was a sprightly woman with white hair who'd been coming to conventions since 1972 in Kansas City. That wasn't so amazing. What was incredible is that Jeanette Riel is 90-something years old. Everything about her is alert, active, and animated. Her mind is quick and her body is agile. Here's a woman who's cared for herself while she took an interest in others. Will you be able to say the same in your nineties?

You can be sure that if you abuse your body, you won't get to use it as long as you'd like.

And there's Henrietta Smith who celebrated her 100th birthday as a guest on the Today Show in New York. She is an avid home gardener and horticulturist and brought many of her favorite potted plants to show the viewers her favorite beauties. When asked how she accounted for her long life, Mrs. Smith smiled and replied, "Oh, I can't leave for the foreseeable future. Who will take care of my flowers?" Make certain you have a reason for living, greater than yourself, that improves the quality of life for everything you touch. Positive self-awareness is understanding how you fit into the big picture in life.

Learning Is a Lifetime Enrollment

Are you also taking care of the mental arena—the thoughts processed by your brain. Are you upbeat and optimistic? It's said that we humans use less than 10 percent of our mental capacity. Most people access only one or two percent of their brain's potential.

What about you? Are you trying to use every ounce of gray matter, or are you allowing life to pass you by while your brain's stuck in neutral? How well are you taking care of your mind and body? Are you enrolled in a lifelong education program? Did you know you can get advanced degrees via the Internet? How literate are you with computers? How many books do you read each month?

Modern Maturity magazine featured an article on Audrey Stubbart, who is a proofreader and columnist for *The Examiner*, a newspaper published six days a week in Independence, Missouri. Ms. Stubbart says, "It's staying busy and keeping interested in things, in what's going on in the world. I'd rather be over-busy than under-busy. I want to keep on living and I want to keep contributing. I'm not in any hurry to get to heaven." Audrey Stubbart works a 40-hour week at an age she'll only give as 100 plus.

If you were honest as you answered the previous questions, you might have been surprised by the pattern that developed. We confess that we were surprised the first time we did this exercise. We had let simple pleasures like sunsets slip away. Looking at how we spend our time is a good way of understanding how few minutes we devote to ourselves—and how often we sacrifice our time to the details of everyday living.

Cynicism Is Contagious

What's even more dangerous to our mental well-being is having negative attitudes which stifle our personal growth and stymie our potential to be successful. Too many people equate being cynical and negative with being chic and sophisticated.

Many of the day-time soaps and talk shows, not to mention the onslaught of evening sitcoms featuring dysfunctional relationships, only enhance this impression. Some people may find Jerry Springer entertaining, just as some enjoy the farcical violence of professional wrestling. The problem is if a 60-second commercial, repeated over time, can influence a buying decision for a product on the part of a consumer, then it stands to reason that a 30- or 60-minute bombardment of the senses by a Jerry Springer free-for-all can influence the perception of the impressionable viewer. Without realizing it, we're being programmed by the programs we watch.

We inhale the negativity that makes us laugh, and we make it our own as surely as if it was oxygen filling our subconscious with each breath.

That's how we set ourselves on the path to self-delusion and defeat. Our greatest strength is in our honest self-awareness, and real achievers acknowledge that it takes work, effort and determination to reach the pay-off. It also takes optimism—and the ability to laugh at our mistakes and applaud our successes, knowing we deserve both.

• • •

Dayna: There is no question that cynicism is contagious. I hear cynicism echo every night on the evening news when the anchor starts with "good evening" and then proceeds to tell us why it's not! But optimism is equally contagious.

I was watching TV recently and happened to catch an old interview with the great mystery writer, Agatha Christie. In addition to being a world-class writer, I soon discovered that she was a world-class optimist.

I learned, among other things, that Agatha Christie was married to a distinguished archeologist who traveled the world for months at a time. When the male interviewer asked her to share the hardships of a woman married to an absentee husband who was obsessed with ancient civilizations, Agatha Christie didn't miss a beat. She retorted, "An archeologist is the best husband any woman could have because the older she gets, the more interested he becomes in her." With one clever reply, Agatha Christie turned cynicism into optimism!

P.S. How about some of you men taking up archeology as a hobby! In our youth-oriented, appearance-conscious society, we women face more challenges than men in accepting ourselves as we get older. Help us appreciate the wisdom of experience that is reflected on our faces.

● ● ●

The Olympic Heroines

During the Olympic Games in Atlanta some years ago, we watched as athletes, one after another, looked deep within themselves and rose to greater heights than they'd ever reached before.

Despite the remarkable achievements of Dan O'Brien, who won gold in the decathlon, or Michael Johnson, who set a new world speed record in the 200 meters, or Carl Lewis, who won an unprecedented ninth gold medal in track and field, the women truly dominated the games.

It is the women who will be remembered most from Atlanta, as the Olympics have moved on to Sydney, Australia, and other global cities in the 21st century.

The real "dream team" in Atlanta was the women's basketball team, the softball and soccer teams, the swimmers, gymnasts, track and field stars, and all the rest of the women, medalists and nonmedalists.

Every one of these winners saw their potential clearly and expected to contribute their best. They didn't allow pain or injuries or a low score in one round to defeat them. They had worked hard. They were aware of their own strengths. And they knew they had earned the right to win.

Champions are open to the alternatives. Did you see the gymnastics exhibition put on after the competition was over?

Kerri Strug didn't allow her injured leg to keep her on the sidelines. She could have sat there watching her teammates and garnered more media attention by focusing on her pain. Instead, she got up and participated. She may not have been able to continue, but she did as much as she could—and she did it without drawing attention to herself. She's a champion.

You couldn't watch the Games without being aware of the growing number of bandages on arms and legs, wrists and ankles, as the grueling tests went on. Jackie Joyner Kersee may have had her thigh taped securely, but she still took bronze in the long jump. Even injured, she wanted to set an example for the fans in the stands. She's a champion in and out of the arena.

Open Your Lenses

Another lesson taught during the Olympics is that champions are open-minded and adaptable to sudden change and adversity. We saw firsthand the camaraderie between the athletes, with no concern for race, color, or creed. Positive self-awareness is accommodating other people's beliefs and cultures and making room for the richness in diversity that thrives in this new, borderless world, which has become like a small village because of the information revolution and the ease of global travel.

How about you? How open-minded are you? Are you still using other people's glasses to bring your life into focus? Are you seeing things in black and white as they did, with no shades of gray? Are you filled with prejudices, the result of other people's fuzzy thinking? Are you satisfied with the color of your skin, your eyes, your hair—or do you want to look like someone else?

High achievers know that the externals—like skin color, hometown, religion, gender, bank balance, and such—aren't the real measures of a person's worth. The big question you have to answer is: How are you going to bring that same unbiased camaraderie into your daily interactions?

Achievers are also empathetic. When you empathize, you feel with another person, instead of sympathizing, which is feeling for them. Empathy is hearing a friend tell you about her root canal and feeling your own jaw ache. Empathetic people automatically draw others to them.

If you want to know how empathetic you are, ask yourself these questions: If I were a man, would I want me for a wife? If I worked for me, would I think I was a good boss? Would I like to have me for a mother?

If I were a young person, would I want me around? Am I constantly talking about the weird people I run into? Did I ever think that others may find me just as strange? Those answers should give you a lot of material for your journal.

And here is the key to self-acceptance—achievers learn how to relax and cope with the trials and tribulations of everyday life. They adapt to conditions. They're not rigid. They go with the flow and don't get upset when things don't go exactly as planned. Very simply, women with self-acceptance don't sweat the small stuff.

They may be very attentive to the details and the basics on a daily basis, but they can color outside the lines, work outside of job descriptions, and deal with a cloudburst, with or without an umbrella.

Action Steps to Discover Your Potential

Now here are a few action steps to help you gain and maintain a healthy self-acceptance:

1. Discover your potential. Revisit your childhood. Spend a day or weekend with the key people in your life, and dust off your childhood memories. Remember what you really loved to do when you were 5 to 15 years of age. All of the talents you began to express as a child are still there, within, awaiting your discovery.

2. Examine your current interests. What do you most enjoy outside of work? What do you most want to do on weekends and vacations? What are your hobbies?

3. Identify your favorite books. Examining your avocational interests might reveal a gem of potential you can apply to your career.

4. Take a natural gifts test. Two organizations—The Ball Foundation and The Johnson O'Connor Foundation—offer natural gifts testing that will identify five to seven of your major talents. Most people spend their lives trying to find out what will make them happy. If we do what we are good at, we will enjoy life a lot more. For information on how to take these revealing talent tests, e-mail, fax or write us in care of the addresses on this book.

5. Increase your reading by 100 percent. Research has proven that people who read the most are the most successful, regardless of their occupations. Read fiction to stimulate your imagination. Read nonfiction to expand your knowledge.

Especially read biographies of women who have overcome hardships to become successful, and read everything you can about electronic networking. Mastering your communication skills will not only help you achieve your goals, it will also free up your time to spend on enjoyable activities. Also, when you read, keep a pocket dictionary beside you. When you see a word that is unfamiliar, look it up on the spot and you'll remember it in the future. There is a direct correlation between high achievement and fulfillment in life, and a rich vocabulary. Verbal and written communication skills are critical for the 21st century woman.

6. *Live in prime time.* Most people watch other people perform on television during prime time, which is 6 to 11 p.m. on weeknights and Saturdays. It is the most expensive time for advertisers because it is the only "free" time we have to live. Never watch TV during dinner. Tape the show for later. Use dinner to have intimate conversations with your loved ones. Spend more evenings talking, reading, taking classes, learning computer skills, writing in your journal, and writing letters. Instead of watching TV, go out to job fairs, entrepreneurial shows, the theater, musical recitals, ethnic restaurants, hobby and craft shows, and engage in community service projects. Life is a participation sport, not a spectator sport!

7. *Do a best and worst exercise.* In your journal, make two columns down the middle of a page, or use two clean facing pages. On one side, write the heading: "I am good at." On the other, "I need improvement in." Now, pick your 10 best traits and 10 most limiting traits and write them down in the appropriate column. Your 10 best might include being punctual, considerate, honest, or discreet. Your 10 most limiting could be activities like gossiping, procrastinating, being late, or eating junk food. Make sure you write down 10.

Next, take the first three traits you don't like about yourself, and plan ways in which you'll change them. Forget the other seven. Just work on the top three to begin with. And while you're at it, thoroughly enjoy each and every one of your assets. Give yourself a little pat on the back for the qualities about you that you feel are good.

8. *Schedule time with "you."* Make an appointment with yourself for yourself. Pull out your appointment calendar, and set aside 15 to 30 precious minutes each day to be alone. During that time, relax and breathe deeply. Meditate as if you were on a mountaintop where no one could reach you. Let your mind float freely. If the phone rings, ignore it. Better yet, unplug it or turn off the ringer before you begin. If you have other things to do, put them aside for a few minutes. Enjoy the gift of time you've given yourself. Remember how much you deserve it.

Anne Morrow Lindbergh, the poet and wife of aviation pioneer Charles Lindbergh, wrote, "If women were convinced that a day off or an hour of solitude was a reasonable ambition, they'd find a way of attaining it. As it is, they feel so unjustified in their demand that they rarely make the attempt."

She continued by saying, "Certain springs are tapped only when we are alone. The artist knows he must be alone to create; the writer, to work out his thoughts; the musician, to compose; the saint, to pray. But women need solitude in order to find again the true essence of themselves."

As you discover your potential by embracing the quality of self-acceptance, and become open to alternatives, you'll also become adaptable to life's changes and ready to accept life's abundance. You'll find your potential is limited only by your imagination. It's the gift you give yourself.

Self-acceptance is the first quality of an achiever—a person who knows who she is, where she's coming from, and how abundant her potential is for a full and rewarding life.

In the next chapter, we'll discuss the second quality, self-confidence, which gives you permission to dream and pursue great dreams.

What Every Woman Needs to Know

Some of the stereotypes placed on women are because the glass ceiling has become a self-fulfilling prophecy. The victim mentality today among women is becoming a self-imposed prison.

It's time to apply your knowledge and skills to achieve your full potential. The opportunities for women to succeed have never been greater than today. Study role models and mentors who have made a difference in the world, rather than "victims of the system," who are harsh reminders that the battle is far from won. Instead of complaining, start training!

Move from Victim to Victor!

What Every Man Needs to Understand

The awareness among women that they can reach their full potential in careers and in creative service to society—while maintaining positive, healthy relationships with significant others and families—is not a fad. It is a permanent trend. It is not a rebellion; it is an awakening. It is not based on economic necessities alone. It is based on enlightenment and growth.

Just as women need to accept that success is not masculine, men need to understand that accepting the new roles of women in society is not "selling out to the competition."

Attempting to discourage women in seeking their destinies today is about the same as refusing to accept the Internet as a place where knowledge and commerce are available.

As women assume more and more top positions as leaders, men can learn from all the significant female role models in their own lives how to balance the natural role of "leading man" with that of "supporting partner."

Chapter 3

•

Deserve to Win

The first step we take toward finding fulfillment and success in our lives is to use the quality of self-acceptance, which teaches us that we have the potential within us to win. We don't have to look for it someplace else. Now it's time to give ourselves permission to succeed by feeling worthy of the best and putting our potential to the test.

We've come to believe that healthy self-esteem is the single most important quality any human being can develop. It comes from the core of your being. It's the equivalent of saying, "I really like myself. I have looked at me and the people around me and my life, and I would rather be me than anyone else in the world." If we don't feel worth loving, it's hard to believe that others love us; instead we tend to see those others as appraisers or judges of our value. Insecurity generates the jealousy, materialism, excessive possessiveness, and compulsion that often ruin caring relationships.

• • •

Denis: During my years of research on healthy self-esteem, I came across a letter from an unknown author that appeared in the book *Glad to Be Me*, written by Dov, Pereta, and Elkins and published by Prentice-Hall (1976). Although the authors of that book never identified the writer of the letter, I'd like to share part of it, since it applies to our discussion.

The words could easily have been written by some inner voice that hides, unseen, in each of us, whispering of our fragile sensitivity and vulnerability to our imagined fears of rejection:

Don't Be Fooled by the Mask I Wear

Don't be fooled by me. Don't be fooled by the face I wear. I wear a mask. I wear a thousand masks—masks that I am afraid to take off. And none of them are me.

Pretending is an art that is second nature to me, but don't be fooled. For my sake, don't be fooled. I give the impression that I am secure, that all is sunny and unruffled within me as well as without, that confidence is my name and coolness is my game, that the water is calm and I am in command, and that I need no one. But don't believe me, please. My surface may seem smooth, but my surface is my mask, my ever-varying and ever-concealing mask.

Beneath lies no smugness, no complacence. Beneath dwells the real me in confusion, in fear, in aloneness. But I hide that. I don't want anybody to know it. I panic at the thought of my weakness and fear being exposed. That's why I frantically create a mask to hide behind—a nonchalant, sophisticated facade—to help me pretend, to shield me from the glance that knows. But such a glance is precisely my salvation, my only salvation, and I know it. That is, if it's followed by acceptance, if it's followed by love.

It's the only thing that can liberate me from myself, from my own self-built prison wall, from the barriers I so painstakingly erect. It's the only thing that will assure me of what I can't assure myself—that I am really something.

Who am I, you wonder? I am someone you know very well. I am every man you meet. I am every woman you meet. I am every child you meet. I am right in front of you. Please. . . love me!

In my original *Psychology of Winning*, I thought that by teaching people about their intrinsic, core values that I was giving them all they needed. It took many years of research and experience with my own career and family to realize something was missing.

Core values usually are taught by nourishing families. As the traditional family has come under siege, positive role models and mentors are in scarce supply. Commercial media bombard our senses ever more insistently with violence, hedonism and other unhealthy forms of escape.

As a result, I believe that self-confidence today is a combination of intrinsic worthiness or self-esteem, combined with self-trust, which is a functional belief in your ability to control what happens to you in a changing, uncertain world.

A sense of worthiness may give you the emotional means to venture forth, but you need self-trust, the sense of competence and control, to believe you can succeed.

If you weren't lucky enough to have a childhood that enriched your self-esteem, you can still gain all you need by learning the life-management attitudes and skills that will help you do successfully what you set out to do. As you begin to experience incremental success, your self-confidence will grow. Empowering you to strive for your goals, self-confidence also continues motivating you, after you've reached your initial objectives, to take more risks and dream more daring dreams.

• • •

Breaking Childhood Barriers

Many people with low self-confidence are evidently trying to avoid or escape from pain. They see themselves as unworthy of success and believe their lives will always be unhappy. They feed the ranks of those who turn to drugs, alcohol, or crime to escape their negative feelings—responses, of course, that only aggravate the problems.

Most psychologists say that gaining or losing confidence starts in infancy, when parents are or aren't able to respond appropriately to a baby's needs and reflect back to the baby that they see, respond to, and accept the baby as he or she really is. Tiny infants can be made to feel that their demands are excessive, burdensome, not worthy of full attention, and can respond by asking for and, worse, expecting less. Comparison is only part of the equation, and this begins as soon as they're old enough to hear parents, peers, and teachers compare them to others.

We remember in our own youth how desperate we were to belong to the "in" group. We felt wonderful when we were accepted, and distraught when we were ignored or rejected. With the greater emphasis today on material and physical appearances, young people seem even more driven to vie for their peers' attention and recognition with unique dress and hairstyles, tattooing and body piercing, as if making an outlandish statement was the key to the good life. However, there's a critical difference between having to prove yourself (wanting to stand out in a crowd to make up for inadequate self-esteem) and seeking to manifest inner worth and value (being our best for the pure exhilaration of excellence). We all struggle with these two forms of expression, regardless of our upbringing.

You can have all the love and positive reinforcement anyone would want from family and friends, and still have negative self-esteem.

On the other side of the coin, we all know people who came from horrendous beginnings, with all of life's challenges thrown at them repeatedly, and still they persevere and win. It's possible to come out of the most dismal beginnings to enormous achievement. As Eleanor Roosevelt said, "A woman is like a tea bag. You never know how strong she is until she gets into hot water."

However, positive encouragement is important for everyone, and we all look to parents and teachers, coaches and husbands, and employers to supplement our feelings of self-worth. But they can't do it for us. Just as self-awareness refers to how we think of ourselves, self-esteem is how we feel about ourselves.

Self-esteem is just what it says—approval that comes from within.

Turning Obstacles into Opportunities

Positive achievers use poverty to spur them on instead of driving them down. Television star Oprah Winfrey talks openly about her traumatic childhood. She didn't get angry. She got out and got ahead. Today she impacts millions of peoples' lives by providing a forum for the sharing of inspirational stories.

So what's the internal difference that makes one person succeed and another lose? It's what's inside you. It's what makes you tick. And who controls that? You do! When you love yourself, when you value your own existence, then and only then will you give yourself permission to go for the gold.

Lucille Ball, one of the most successful women in show business, said, "Love yourself first, and everything else falls into line. You really have to love yourself to get anything done in this world."

Dr. Elizabeth Kubler-Ross, who has done marvelous work with the dying and now with children who have AIDS, has written, "The ultimate lesson all of us have to learn is unconditional love, which includes not only others, but ourselves."

The Woman Behind the Mask

The work of developing a healthy self-esteem is particularly difficult for women because our culture teaches us to put aside our own feelings and needs to serve others.

In a speech to the management of Estée Lauder cosmetic company, author Marianne Williamson pinpointed the problem. She feels that women's attitudes about make-up and clothes basically say, "Give me a place to hide. Be the mask. Do it for me. If I can find the make-up that looks right or the clothes that look right, then I won't have to deal with who I am."

She further pointed out that the exterior camouflage works only until a woman is 35 or 40, and then it becomes more difficult to hide who we are. Life leaves its imprint on our faces. The long days and late nights help to turn our hair gray.

How do we feel about ourselves then, when we begin to age? Marianne Williamson urges every woman to consider herself more beautiful as she ages, as her inner beauty shines through.

As she said, "Now we're looking inside to find out who we really are because what we've been through, our so-called failures as well as our successes, and our greatest education, has been our life experience. We must show we are out of hiding, we are expressing, we are transforming!"

You Are an Original

Do you know that you are as unique as a snowflake? No one else on this planet—not even your identical twin—has your same fingerprints, lip prints, voice pattern, or a brain that works exactly like yours. You're one of a kind—and that makes you special from the day you're born.

It's sometimes hard to accept this when all the time you were growing up, you had people telling you not to interrupt, or that you were too old or too young to do something, or that children are to be "seen and not heard."

After a dozen or more years, the constant implication that you're not old enough, smart enough, capable enough, experienced enough—or anything else enough—begins to seep into your subconscious.

Before long, you find you've bought into other people's opinions and made them your own. During the troubled teen years, it's easy to go down the loser's path and become inwardly convinced of your own inadequacies.

Academy-award winning actress Sally Field said, "I was raised to sense what someone wanted me to be and be that kind of person. It took me a long time not to judge myself through someone else's eyes." Eleanor Roosevelt admonished, "Nobody can make you feel inferior without your consent."

• • •

Dayna: I have a great respect for women who not only roll with the punches, but also hold their ground in difficult situations.

I recently heard a story about a flight attendant who had the self-confidence to stand up to the loudest personality among professional athletes.

Apparently Dennis Rodman, at that time with the Chicago Bulls, was sitting in the first-class section of an airplane that was ready to take off in Chicago. As the flight attendant made her way down the aisle, she noticed that Dennis Rodman had not yet fastened his seat belt.

As she is required to do, she politely said, "Please fasten your seatbelt, sir."

Dennis Rodman looked up at her with one of his intimidating stares, thumped his chest, and proclaimed, "Superman doesn't need a seatbelt!"

With her self-esteem clearly intact, the flight attendant kept her composure and calmly responded, "Well, superman doesn't need an airplane, either."

While Dennis Rodman fastened his seatbelt, the two exchanged smiles and the flight attendant continued her duties, knowing that a little self-confidence went a long way in defusing what could have been a very uncomfortable situation.

P.S. What may seem cool and macho (to some of you men) on the basketball court doesn't always work in real life. All we're asking for, as Rodney Dangerfield says, is a little respect. If you can acknowledge your own self-worth and know that, deep down inside, you are a unique and lovable human being, you won't need to impress us. We love you just the way you are.

● ● ●

Roll with the Punches

Your independent thinking has to hold firm in the workplace. The woman who gets ahead doesn't allow herself to be sidetracked by her detractors. As CEO of Enron Development, Rebecca Mark handles international business ventures for Enron Corporation in Houston, Texas.

She told *Fortune* magazine that women, especially, need to loosen up and roll with the punches. "You can't take things that people say personally. If you do, your confidence goes down, your ego gets in the way, and you don't get the work done." She's proof that when you believe in your own abilities, no one else's opinion can bring you down.

Embrace the Unfamiliar

So what can you do if you have low self-esteem? The obvious answer is: change. But that can be easier said than done. Many of us tend to fight change with a vengeance. It's frightening to think about changing our internal, self-defeating attitudes. They're familiar and comfortable. Change is like getting out of a warm bed and putting your feet down on the cold floor in the morning.

It's not pleasant, but it must be done. Losers fear change and do everything possible to avoid it. Achievers embrace change. They live their lives as if the thrift shop donation truck is outside, with its engine running, waiting to make a pick-up. Out go the old behaviors, the out-of-date technology, and the antique ways of thinking.

Break Old Patterns

In their place come new skills, ideas and sensitivities to take their place.

For many of us, the tremendous strides in technology have created stress instead of relieving it. Too often we base our self-esteem on the competence with which we function in the world. Suddenly, there are new machines to operate, new systems to learn, and new concepts to understand. Unfortunately, the older we are, the more we tend to step back and view the new developments with suspicion.

We all know someone—maybe a mother or grandmother—who would rather hang clothes on the line on a cold winter day than learn how to run a dryer. Or who complains that no one calls her but refuses to figure out how an answering machine works. Or who says there's nothing good to watch on standard television but refuses to install cable. They'll tell you they mistrust these new-fangled contraptions.

51

Why switch to e-mail when the post office is available? Why get a microwave when the stove is working fine? Why go on the Internet when there's a library full of books on the corner? Why own a DVD player when movies are meant to be shown in theaters? The list goes on and on. The truth is, each modern improvement requires us to re-train and learn new ways of doing things. Old patterns have to be broken and reestablished.

The American writer, Doris Schwerin, said, "Sometimes a life, like a house, needs renovating, the smell of new wood, new rooms in the heart, unimagined until one begins the work. One rebuilds because the structure deserves a renewing."

And the French feminist writer, Simone De Beauvoir, echoed that thought when she wrote, "Change your life today. Don't gamble on the future, act now, without delay."

Why do we fight change so much? Change makes us nervous and disoriented. We have a feeling of losing control. In our knowledge and competence, we find strength and confidence. New ways of doing things mean new things to learn—and the possibility of making a mistake, of appearing foolish in someone's eyes.

It's said that the vast majority of people who own VCRs have never learned to set the time, so the clock blinks 12:00 perpetually. The answer is to find an eight-year-old. Children understand they don't know everything. They expect to be learning constantly. So what we consider a challenge, they look at as a normal part of growing up. Today, if you're putting your toe into the new technology, ask a child to teach you, and you'll learn more quickly.

Ask for Help

If you have a deep desire to change, you'll find out how to do it. All it takes to begin is to ask for help—which is the most powerful bond you can forge with another person.

Who's going to turn down your request? Walk up to someone and say, "Can you help me?" Few will turn you down. It makes us feel good to help someone. It replenishes our confidence in our own abilities.

It gives our egos a little boost to know we're in a position to be of service. Try asking for help, and don't be surprised when you get it. It works every time.

One reason many of us have low self-esteem is that we concentrate on our failures instead of our successes. We babble on to ourselves—and anyone else who will listen—about the things we haven't done, the places we haven't been, the tests we failed, the jobs we lost, the pounds we didn't lose, and all our other failures, big and small, that we've made the milestones in our lives.

Sometimes our failures are the result of trying to live up to external standards set by others. Sometimes the goals we have set for ourselves are too unrealistic.

For instance, if your parents have tried to turn you into a lawyer—when you really want to design costumes for the theater—then, if you're going to be happy, you're going to be seen as a failure in your family's eyes.

Other times, the goals we set are too high and are impossible to reach. If you were to decide at 15 that you want to become a world-class gymnast—even though you're six feet tall and weigh 150 pounds—the chances are pretty good you're setting yourself up for failure. Not only are gymnasts tiny in size, they also begin training in preschool.

This is a goal you probably won't be able to achieve. You're setting yourself up for a fall, and your self-esteem is going down with you.

What you want to do is be certain that you don't let the inevitable life disappointments overshadow all the things you *have* accomplished—and *can* accomplish in the future.

• • •

Don't Live on "Someday I'll"

A poem by Denis Waitley

There is an island fantasy,
A "Someday I'll" we'll never see
Where violence stops and warring ceases
Our jobs are secure with guaranteed pay increases
That "Someday I'll" where problems end
Where every call is from a friend
Where children are sweet and already grown
Where every nation can go it alone
Where we all retire at forty-one
Playing Backgammon in the island sun
Most unhappy people look to tomorrow
To erase today's pain and sorrow
They put happiness on "layaway"
And struggle through another bad day
But happiness cannot be sought
It can't be earned and it can't be bought
Life's most important revelation
Is that the journey counts more than the destination
Happiness is where you are right now
Pushing your pencil or pushing your plow
The fear of results is procrastination
The joy of today is a celebration
You can go through life trudging mile after mile
But you'll never set foot on "Someday I'll"
When you've paid all your dues and put in your time
Out of nowhere comes another mountain to climb
From this day forward make it your vow
Take "Someday I'll" and make it your Now!

• • •

Don't become one of those people with "permanent potential"—someone who's favorite verb is "going to," one of those who spend their time on "Someday I'll." "Someday I'll write a book. Someday I'll lose weight. Someday I'll travel to China and see the Great Wall." Meanwhile, in truth, they're mired in a rut that they're digging deeper and deeper.

Make promises to yourself that you can keep. The aviator and writer, Beryl Markham, said, "Nothing is as inexorable as a promise to your pride."

Facing Your Fears

You can't stop smoking as a present to someone else. You won't lose weight to please your spouse. Jenny Craig, who founded the highly successful chain of weight-loss clinics, admitted that: "Self-love is the only weight loss aid that really works in the long run." The promise you make to yourself is the only promise you can be sure you'll keep. It's the only promise that will give you the courage to conquer your fear of change.

Long after Brooke Knapp was married, she realized that the boundaries of her world were very narrow. She'd been protected and sheltered as a child, and as an adult she was fearful of so many things that it was hard to fully participate in life. She decided to face down her fears and break out of the shell that had been wrapped around her. More than anything, she was afraid of flying, and she was afraid of speaking in front of a group. These are recognized as two of the most common fears among Americans today. But Brooke had determined to break free.

To meet her fears head-on, she decided to take flying lessons. Today, Brooke holds multiple speed records piloting private planes. She has flown around the world across the poles, instead of around the equator. She talked the Russians into allowing her to fly from Moscow to Bejing. Not only that, today she's a highly successful business-woman, an acknowledged expert in the aviation industry, and a professional speaker. Brooke says that if she could do it for herself, you can do it too.

Oprah Winfrey could have been talking about Brooke Knapp when she said, "I have a lot of things to prove to myself. One is that I can live my life fearlessly."

Nothing is as frightening and as fatal to your dreams as fear of the unknown. Nothing dispels fear faster than making the unknown familiar.

"Dispelling Fear" Journal Exercise

Use your journal as you begin to learn new things. Here's a two-step exercise you'll find helpful.

On one page, write today's date and make a list of five things you've never done before. These should be things you've avoided because you were afraid of appearing foolish or you were physically afraid.

They don't have to represent major, life-threatening fears. You might choose eating an artichoke, or riding on a roller coaster, or having dinner in a nice restaurant all by yourself, or offering to read in church on Sunday, or singing in a karaoke bar, or changing the tire on your car. Leave room on the page to write in the results of step two.

As you've probably imagined, step two is to try all the things that would have intimidated you before. Don't give yourself time to get nervous. Just go for it. Then write down what you've tried and whether or not you succeeded. Laugh at yourself if you got it wrong. Applaud yourself if you got it right.

Give yourself an extra pat on the back if you had to ask for help and got it. And above all, love yourself—with all your faults and achievements—just for being alive.

Self-Esteem Must Be Learned

When psychotherapist Linda Tschirhart Sanford and her partner Mary Ellen Donovan wrote the book *Women and Self-Esteem*, their friends would refer to it as "The Blind Leading the Blind." Linda Sanford understood this attitude. She said, "I grew up with low self-esteem, and perhaps the most important thing we learned from writing this book is that there is really nothing innate or God-given about self-esteem. It has to be learned along the way."

Colette Dowling, in *The Perfect Woman*, suggests that for many women "enoughness" is the perfection we aspire to. We go through life muttering "If only's"—"If only I were prettier, wealthier, more educated, had more experience, was more organized, laughed more, was more serious," and on and on. We use these excuses to fill in the empty spaces in our lives. Some of us punish ourselves for our lack of perfection with eating disorders, drug and alcohol abuse, exhaustion, and all the other stress-related symptoms of trying to be Superwoman.

The writer Annie Lamott says, "Perfectionism is the voice of the oppressor, the enemy of the people. It will keep you cramped and insane your whole life." You will become so driven toward perfection that you will cut yourself off from your true feminine nature. In *Addiction to Perfection: The Still Unravished Bride*, Marion Woodman says, "to move toward perfection is to move out of life, or, what is worse, never to enter it."

• • •

Deborah: I know what it's like to feel that no matter what you do, it is never enough. Before I met my husband, I was pursuing a degree in psychology, but then left school to be with him. A tennis player, he had just come off the professional circuit to manage a regional sports club. After we married, I poured myself into being the best wife and mother possible. I decorated and cleaned the house, cooked meals every night, took care of our young son, Jake, while helping my husband's business by managing the tennis proshop, marketing club memberships to the community, and organizing and catering tennis socials. My life as a "superwoman" worked for a while, but about three years into the marriage I began to sense something was missing. I realized I was living a life that wasn't my own. Where had my dreams gone? Had I somehow forgotten them? Did I ever really have any to begin with?

I yearned to get out and explore life away from the tennis club and my family. I envisioned going back to school and perhaps starting my own business to feel a sense of independence and personal freedom. But my husband was adamant about my being home every night and working with him during the day. Some nights I cried myself to sleep.

I became guilt-ridden and began cursing myself for having these feelings of betrayal toward my family. But I was really betraying myself. I masked my unhappiness and frustration by trying even harder to be a good wife and mother. I became obsessive and perfectionistic about my appearance and weight, and developed a few unhealthy eating behaviors.

My frustration had turned inward because I lacked the self-esteem to assert my wants and desires. I couldn't give myself permission to be happy.

Finally, at the end of my rope, I mustered the courage to enroll in an evening psychology class at a local educational institute, and I started teaching aerobics classes at a community recreation facility. I experienced a newly found sense of self—one of competence and control. For so long I had served the needs of others, while sacrificing my own. I began to feel that I, too, deserved to win in life.

My husband didn't approve of my new independence. He felt threatened by my self-confidence and began asserting more control. Our marriage came down to a final ultimatum of either commiting myself 100 percent to our partnership of running the sports club for the next 10 years—waiting until I was 40 to do what I wanted—or the marriage was over. I couldn't bare to live a life that didn't allow me to explore and develop my own potential. I deserved more.

The divorce was final over 12 years ago. My former husband is happily remarried, and I am on good terms with both him and his wife. We have shared joint custody of Jake over the years, which, although extremely challenging at times, has worked out positively for all of us. I am still single and loving my independence while raising Jake, now a teenager and in his last year of living at home before going off to college. Because I was able to feel that I deserved to be winning in life, I most certainly am.

P.S. I think it is important for men, as well as women, to encourage the growth and development of your spouse, significant other, or anyone you are in a relationship with. Though it can feel threatening to your sense of security at times, it ultimately will free you to become more of who you are, thus bringing you more happiness and fulfillment.

● ● ●

Internal vs. External Worth

Writer Linda Henley said, "So many of us define ourselves by what we have, what we wear, what kind of house we live in, and what kind of car we drive. If you think of yourself as the woman in the Cartier watch and the Hermes scarf, a house fire will destroy not only your possessions but your self."

And Gail Sheehy, the author of *New Passages*, wrote, "Would that there were an award for people who come to understand the concept of enough. Good enough. Successful enough. Thin enough. Rich enough. Socially responsible enough. When you have self-respect, you have enough—and when you have enough, you have self-respect."

Let the "enoughs" in your life be tempered by the possible and attainable. Don't think it isn't "enough" unless you win a beauty contest or a Pulitzer Prize. You don't have to have Oprah's money to show a little of Mother Teresa's compassion for others. Everything in moderation—strive for what is enough for you, and that's probably going to be more than enough for those who love you.

Linda Sanford points out that many women downplay their best qualities because they don't feel they're worth anything. We feel that if we have a particular talent or ability, it probably isn't very important.

Furthermore, a woman will admit that's she's a good wife, a good mother, a good worker, a fun and attractive person with a good personality, and then she'll add, "but I'm 10 pounds overweight." Even though she acknowledges her good qualities, she continues to focus on the flaws. She still sees herself, first and foremost, as a failure because she's not model-thin.

Women suffer from depression twice as often as men, according to the American Psychological Association's Task Force on Women. We sell ourselves short and stunt our potential because we think we don't have what it takes.

We allow ourselves to wallow in self-pity, our self-esteem plummets, and we're incapable of dreaming bright dreams.

Power of Positive Self-Talk

Since a healthy self-esteem is essential for every winner, we need to know how we can improve it. What can we do to turn around a bad attitude and learn to love ourselves?

Perhaps the most important key to permanent enhancement of self-confidence is the practice of positive self-talk. When monitored on bio-feedback equipment, there's been a positive interaction between spoken words and body functions.

Thoughts can raise and lower body temperature; secrete hormones; relax muscles and nerve endings; dilate and restrict muscles, nerve endings, and arteries; and lower or raise pulse rate. This is pretty convincing proof that we need to control the language we use on ourselves.

Recently the American Heart Association and the medical journal *Hypertension* published the results of a study conducted in Oakland, California. One group of men and women with high blood pressure was taught to practice Transcendental Meditation twice daily. They repeated the same word or phrase over and over again for 20 minutes, concentrating on nothing else. A second group was given a routine stress-reduction method called progressive muscle relaxation.

A third control group was lectured on diet, exercise, and general health.

At the end of the three months, the men and women who meditated lowered their blood pressure twice as much as those practicing the muscle relaxation method. The control group showed no change. American medical science seems to be proving what other cultures have known for centuries—the mind has a profound effect on the body.

Humility without Humiliation

Too often, we show our lack of self-esteem when someone pays us a compliment. A compliment should be considered a little gift that's been bestowed upon us. Instead, many women belittle themselves, in effect throwing the gift back at the giver. Someone says, "That dress looks great!" And instead of a simple "Thank you," we say, "Oh, this old thing? It's ready for the rag bag!"

When you say, "Dinner was delicious. I wish I could cook like you," how many times do you hear back, "It was nothing—just something I threw together."

You compliment the PTA speaker by telling her, "You gave a terrific talk at the meeting today," and she tells you, "I was so nervous, I can't remember what I said."

Then women wonder why we don't get more compliments and why we're not more appreciated. Perhaps, because we don't appreciate ourselves, it's difficult for anyone else to appreciate us. We don't believe that we deserve to be praised. We want the brass ring, but we don't trust ourselves to reach for it.

When you use positive self-talk, you are using statements as a self-confidence affirmation. Successful people rarely use negative statements such as, "I coulda, woulda, shoulda." They don't say, "I'll try" or "I wish." Instead, they say, "I can, I will, I'm better, I'll get it right, I look forward to, I'll do it." They use this constructive self-talk every day.

Your self-talk doesn't have to be about your dreams and personal goals. You can just as easily use it to achieve business goals or athletic goals. You can use it to direct yourself to whatever you want to accomplish.

———————•———————

Scott Adams, the cartoonist who draws the wildly popular "Dilbert," uses another version of the positive self-talk
affirmation technique. Instead of saying the words aloud,
he writes them down 15 times every day. His affirmations
have included "I will become a syndicated cartoonist" and
"I will be the best cartoonist on the planet."

When he was preparing to take his GMAT test to get into
business school, his affirmation was that he wanted to get a 94
on the exam. When the results came in, he had earned exactly 94. That's when he learned never to limit his dreams. He
could just as easily have dreamed of a perfect score.

Words to Forget:	*Words to Remember:*
I can't	I can
I'll try	I will
I have to	I choose to
Should have	Will do
If only	Next time
Problem	Opportunity
Difficult	Challenging
Stressed	Motivated
I, me, my	You, your
Yes, but	Yes, lets do it
Hate	Love

Take a Reality Check

To give yourself a self-confidence reality check, ask
yourself these questions:
- Would I rather be somebody else? If so, why?
- Do I internalize criticism—that is, take things per-
  sonally—rather than seek to learn from criticism?
- Do I feel guilty when I indulge in a "selfish" activity?
- Am I comfortable when others praise or compliment me?

- Do I ridicule myself too often in front of others, or do I speak about myself with respect?
- Is the exterior of my lifestyle more important to me than my inner values?
- Is making a good impression on others more important than being true to myself?
- Do I constantly have to prove my worth by my outer achievements?

Make Self-Esteem a Priority

If you conclude from your answers that your self-confidence is lacking, set as your number one goal "develop better self-esteem." Make it a priority in your life. No matter who you are or what your family background, you are special, unique, and irreplaceable. Engage in activities that will help you recognize your individual talents, abilities, and opportunities for success. Associate with people who will encourage you toward, and then applaud, your accomplishments.

You can value yourself without reducing the value of others. You can appreciate yourself as a person capable of beauty, honesty, sound values, achievement, and healthy relationships—without worshipping yourself or causing yourself to be placed at the center of your universe.

Self-confidence also need not imply that you consider yourself to be at the center of anyone else's universe. Self-confidence is not an exercise in vying to be Number One. Don't confuse having high self-esteem with being egocentric. Esteem and ego are worlds apart.

Esteem says: "I'm valuable." Ego says: "I'm the most valuable of all." Esteem says: "What I say is important." Ego says: "Only what *I* say is important." Esteem says: "I can look at others and value them, because I value myself." Ego says: "Others must look at me and value me." Esteem says: "I am a creation of God and am truly unique." Ego says: "God should have stopped after creating me!" Having healthy self-esteem and keeping your ego within bounds are both possible.

It's better to set internal standards for success rather than to live by comparison. When you compare yourself to others less successful than yourself, you run the risk of an overly inflated ego, which requires a lot of time and energy to maintain. If you compare yourself unfavorably with others, you may become frustrated.

Executives, athletes, and entertainers often belittle their efforts by comparing their accomplishments to the giants in the field who have done better than they.

"Replay Your Accomplishments" Journal Exercise

Make a list in your journal of every talent you have, however small, and every goal you have accomplished that's been important to you. You'll likely discover that some of your greatest reasons for self-confidence are buried in past experience.

No matter what you do or what position you occupy, give it your best effort—because you are worth your best effort. Others may accept us and make us feel we belong. Others may be lavish in their praise of who and what we are, but if we have violated our conscience or sense of value, we will not feel worthy. There is no opinion so critical as the one you hold of yourself.

"Deserve to Win" Action Steps

Here are some action steps to help you deserve to win and build more self-confidence:

1. *Greet others with a smile and look them directly in the eye.* A smile and direct eye contact convey confidence born of self-respect.

2. Answer the phone pleasantly, whether at work or at home. In placing calls to others, give your name before asking to speak to the party you've called. Leading with your name underscores that a person of value is making the call.

3. When you make a mistake, are ridiculed, or are rejected, choose to view your errors as an opportunity to learn. View a failure as the conclusion of one performance, not the end of your entire career! Don't make excuses. Own up to your failures. A failure is something you have done, not necessarily something you will do again, and definitely not something you are!

4. Always say "Thank you" when you are given a compliment. Don't downplay or sidestep a compliment. The ability to accept, or receive, is the universal mark of an individual with solid self-esteem.

5. Don't make your problems the centerpiece of your conversations. Talk affirmatively about positive aspects of your life and the forward progress you are trying to make.

6. Become aware of your negative thinking. Notice how often you complain. When you hear yourself criticize something or someone (including yourself), say to yourself, "Bad seeds! That's not like you!" And find a way to be helpful instead of critical.

7. Don't constantly talk about yourself. People who trumpet their own exploits or demand special favors or service are desperate for attention. In fact, they are likely to be people of marginal self-esteem who are attempting to build themselves up in the eyes of others because they don't perceive themselves as already worthy of respect.

8. Increase your productive activity level. During bad times and depressing moments, when self-esteem is hurting, we tend to sit around and engage in "analysis to paralysis." Instead, do something productive.

Do Something!

Get out of your chair, get out of your office or room, and get into an activity that at least requires physical activity. It is difficult to be depressed and active at the same time. The late Malcolm Forbes said, "Vehicles in motion use their own generators to charge their own batteries." You can't recharge your battery when you're parked in the garage—unless you're a golf cart! Forbes believed the important thing is never to say die, until you're dead, and he lived that example to the hilt.

As we said at the beginning of this chapter, self-esteem may give you the emotional courage to begin, but self-confidence only comes with self-trust that you are competent enough to control the outcomes in your life. This must be learned through experience. Take on a specific project, do it well, complete it, and get the accompanying reward and motivation for having been successful.

Discovering your potential and deserving to win are important first steps on the road to success. In the next chapter, we'll talk about how to dare to choose and take the calculated risk to make success happen *for* you, rather than wait and see what happens *to* you.

Ten Self-Affirming Beliefs

1. I control my thoughts, emotions and actions—and I direct them to improve the quality of my health, relationships, work and life.

2. I am a good, valuable, and worthy person.

3. I am fully capable of achieving the goals I set for myself today.

4. I trust my abilities and my judgments in taking risks that will test my limits, and I am willing to live with the consequences and rewards of my decisions.

5. I am responsible for the values by which I live.

6. I learn from problems and setbacks, and through them I can find opportunities for improvement and growth.

7. My spirit, mind, and body are a powerful team, which I set free to excel.

8. I am my own best friend and coach. Whan I talk to myself, I am encourageing, supportive, and respectful.

9. Every day I am becoming more knowledgeable, more aware, more curious, more caring, more abaptable, more successful and more in control.

10. Regardless of what happens in my life, I have decided to be happy.

What Every Woman Needs to Know

- Believing that you deserve success, in advance, is like getting your passport for global travel. You can't leave home without it!
- The deep-down, inside-the-skin feeling of your own worth—regardless of your background, appearance, or current status—is the key to motivation. Without belief in what you *can* do, there is no reason or energy to try.

What Every Man Needs to Understand

- Men with healthy self-esteem are not threatened or jealous when the woman they live with or work with gain power or prestige.
- In order to be loved, you first must be lovable. You cannot possess love. You must set those you love free and risk whether that love will return.

Chapter 4

———————•———————

Decide to Excel

The positive characteristics of an achiever are the building blocks which take you from where you are to where you want to be. As important as what you do is the mindset you use to do it, and that's what you'll discover in this chapter.

• • •

Denis: We've talked about being aware of your potential and having the self-confidence to go after what you want because you have self-esteem based upon self-trust. Now we move on to the next step—taking control of your choices and actions. To achieve that, you need the characteristic of self-determination.

When you have the characteristic of self-determination, you take the responsibility for everything you do. This is a very important theme because losers "let" it happen and winners "make" it happen. When you're able to understand this attitude, you'll have the key to decision-making, and you'll be able to decide easily and effectively which goals you want to pursue. The first thing a winner realizes is that she has the potential to win. Then she discovers she's in control of making it happen.

All the images and all the goals she has set are achieved because she realizes that she's at the wheel, steering herself to her own destination. My own life creed is a "Do-It-With-God, Do-It-For-Others, Do-It-To-Myself" program. Self-determination as it relates to the psychology of winning is synonymous with responsibility, and high achievers take full responsibility for their own lives.

• • •

Taking Responsibility for Your Life

When many people consider self-determination, they think of gritting their teeth and bearing down. We view self-determination as simply taking control of your life. Not so much the kind of control as in staying cool and collected under pressure, or getting a grip on yourself, or not getting angry when something annoys you. The woman who has self-control doesn't yell at her children when they track mud on the newly waxed floor, she doesn't blow up at her co-workers when their mistake has cost her time and labor, and she doesn't take it out on the dry cleaner when he has ruined her favorite coat.

That may be the common perception of self-control, but in the vocabulary of the *Psychology of Winning for Women*, we've expanded the meaning to the more appropriate term, *self-determination*. Self-determination is taking responsibility for yourself and your actions. It's knowing that what you do is directly responsible for the results you achieve. Truly successful people take responsibility for what happens in their lives—both good and bad.

All of life is a "do-it-yourself" project. We're constantly given alternatives, and we pick and choose among the opportunities to shape our own destinies.

We Cause Our Own Effects

Some people put their faith in luck or magical notions, gurus and cults, to shape the outcome of their lives. But that's just another way of passing off the responsibility for their actions. You are who you are because of what you have chosen to do. It may sometimes help to be in the right place at the right time, but ultimately—either through positive action or sheer laziness—you choose the place and the time.

There's a very definite "cause and effect" correlation between what we do and what happens to us when we do it. We learn it as babies. When infants want attention, they cry and someone picks them up and feeds them. They laugh and people make a fuss over them. Then as toddlers, they learn that a tantrum gets an instant reaction, and if they can manage to have that tantrum in a public place, they'll probably get what they want, just to keep them quiet. These are powerful lessons.

$$\bullet \quad \bullet \quad \bullet$$

Dayna: We all have felt controlled by other people at different points in our life. As children, we may feel that our parents or teachers control our destiny. As adults, we may feel like a slave to our spouse, our boss, or even to our children. Whenever I question my ability to cause my own effects in life, I remember a story that my father has told about me for over twenty years. It is as timely now as it was when I was eleven months old. It rings true to any parent who believes, as I do, that control begins at birth.

I was sitting in my high chair for dinner one evening, enjoying a bowl of banana pudding. My father decided I should eat something less sweet and more nutritious, so he decided to warm a jar of strained squash for my next culinary pleasure. He tasted it to test the temperature. It nearly made him gag, but he knew it was good for me. He held the little curved spoon out and gently entreated, "Open up, honey. Daddy has some yummy squash for you." I stared coldly at him and clamped my mouth shut in passive defiance.

Although I was unable to speak, he said my look suggested, "Go ahead, fatso. If you like it, you eat it." Feeling in total control of the situation, he simply pressed my cheeks firmly with two fingers, forcing my mouth open. He then neatly inserted the spoonful of squash into my mouth and quietly but sternly ordered, "Go on, swallow it, it's good for you." I spit it out all over his face, hair and necktie. I had decided at age eleven months that I didn't like strained squash!

To this day I do not like butternut squash or zucchini, and my own two children, Alex and Alissa, constantly remind me of children's ability to exercise their own free will and impose their unique standard of living!

P.S. It is important for men to understand that trying to control situations or force certain behaviors is not going to work—especially in the family setting. Unfortunately, you men have been burdened over the years with the pressures and responsibilities of being "king of the castle." Women now are beginning to share this role alongside you. We must learn to work as a team to give our children the roots from which to mature into responsible adults, as well as wings in which to soar to their highest potential.

● ● ●

As adults, successful human beings realize that everything we do in life is by our own volition. We choose to keep on living. We decide to do something because it's profitable to those we care about and good for ourselves. Some of us choose evil. Most try to choose good. Some choose pleasure without purpose. Others choose purpose, which brings the added benefits of pleasure and well-being.

No one has to work. There are government handouts that will sustain you—or you can mooch off family and friends, or live in the streets. You can choose revolving unemployment. You don't have to pay taxes. You have the option of going to prison for tax evasion.

You don't have to fix dinner, have children, or even get up in the morning. It's up to you to decide what you want to do, not out of compulsion, but because it's beneficial to you.

You can make the best choices among the alternatives available to help you toward your goals. So the high achievers in life—and the real successes—are wide open to choices and constantly look for a better way to live.

Take the Credit or the Blame for Who You Are

Nonachievers are the frightened ones, the people who tend to doubt, mistrust, and are unable to make a decision. They let life carry them along like a leaf in the stream and shrug their shoulders philosophically, while muttering "que sera sera"— "what will be, will be." Their negative mantra is, "Don't blame me! It's not my fault. I couldn't help it!"

This reluctance to take the blame is as old as the human race, but it stays perennially young through constant use. Eve ate the forbidden fruit and blamed it all on the serpent.

She was the first to offer the excuse "The Devil made me do it!" Then Adam ate the forbidden apple, and what did he do? He pointed his finger and turned the blame on Eve and God. "The woman who You put here with me, made me do it." Obviously if God hadn't created them, none of this would have happened.

How many times do you hear people blame their parents, their government, the economy, or the current welfare laws for the mess they're in? The fault lies with the company they work for and the bosses they report to. If it weren't for their husband or their children, they'd get the job done. Their parents are to blame because they didn't love them enough or loved them too much. They never look inside themselves to find the answers. Instead, they point the finger at their surroundings. It's always easier and more convenient to assume there's an external cause for an internal problem.

The fiercely-independent and outspoken actress, Katherine Hepburn, wrote, "We are taught you must blame your father, your sisters, your brothers, the school, the teachers—you can blame anyone, but never blame yourself. It's never your fault. But it's always your fault, because if you wanted to change, you're the one who has got to change. It's as easy as that."

The trend toward avoiding personal responsibility is evident when we observe the proliferation of lawsuits after a preventable tragedy. A child dies in a swimming pool accident and the parents sue the company that installed the pool. It's far more comfortable to lash out at an innocent third party than to accept the crushing responsibility for taking your eyes off the youngster for a few minutes.

One of the lessons drummed into our heads growing up is that God's unfailing boomerang will always get you, sooner or later. "What goes around, comes around"—you can count on it.

What you do today, good or bad, will surely come back to you in the long run. The lie you tell today will return to haunt you or hurt you someday. And conversely, the good deed you do will ultimately help you or heal you somehow.

● ● ●

Denis: One of the best-kept secrets of total success is that our rewards in life will depend on the quality and amount of contribution we make. We want to cut taxes, take the great risk, and build our own destinies, and at the same time we want more security and safety provided by our government. We plead for more protections from crime but demand less interference in our social habits. But we can't have it both ways. If we want results, we must pay the price. Responsibility needs to be redefined and retaught to this and all upcoming generations. To attain emotional security, each of us must learn to develop two critical capacities: the ability to live with uncertainty and the ability to delay immediate gratification in favor of long-range goals.

As the father of six children, I know from experience that the greatest gifts that parents can give their children (and that leaders can give their teams) are roots and wings, instead of loot and things. Roots of core values that will keep them strong through environmental storms, and wings of responsibility that will teach them how to rely on themselves to gain independence. When those roots and wings are missing, the results are very disturbing.

In my parenting and leadership seminars, I tell a true story about a young couple who invited me to their home for dinner. They were both very intelligent, with advanced degrees, but had opted for a "child-centered home," so their five-year-old son, Bradford, whom I silently named "Bradford the Barbarian," would have everything at his disposal to become a winner out in the competitive world. What many parents don't realize is that by waiting hand and foot on their children so their children won't have to wait, they are tying their hands and feet so they can't grow into self-reliant adults.

When I arrived at their driveway in front of a fashionable two-story Tudor home at the end of a cul-du-sac, I should have sensed what was in store for me. I stepped on his Mighty Morphin Power Rangers getting out of the car and was greeted by, "Watch where you're walking, Mister, or you'll have to buy me a new one!"

Bradford made Macauly Caulkin and Dennis the Menace seem like members of the Vienna Boys' Choir! Entering the front door, I instantly discovered that this was

Bradford's place, not his parents'. The furnishings, it appeared, were originally of fine quality. I thought I recognized an Ethan Allen piece that had suffered from Mortal Kombat and Terminator 5.

We attempted to have a cup of cider in the family room, but Bradford was busy ruining his new CD-ROM PC with a hand drill he must have seen on Home Improvement. Trying to find a place to sit down was like hopping on one foot through a mine field, blindfolded. Bradford got to eat first, in the living room, of course, so he wouldn't be lonely. I nearly dropped my hot cup of cider in my lap in shock when his parents brought out a high chair that was designed like a jet fighter plane's ejection seat with four legs and straps. (I secretly visualized a 20-millimeter cannon shell, strapped to a skyrocket under the seat, with a two-second fuse.)

He was five years old and had to be strapped in a high chair to get through one meal! As we started our salads in the dining room, which was an open alcove adjoining the living room, young Bradford dumped his dinner on the carpet and proceeded to pour his milk on top of it to ensure that the peas and carrots would go deep into the shag fibers. His mother entreated, "Brad, sweetie, don't do that. Mommy wants you to grow up strong and healthy like Daddy. I'll get you some more yummy dinner while Daddy cleans your little accident up!"

While they were occupied, Bradford had unfastened his seatbelts, scrambled down from his perch, and joined me in the dining room, helping himself to the olives and tomatoes in my salad. "I think you should wait for your own dinner," I said politely, removing his hand from my salad.

He swung his leg up to kick me in the knee, but my old ex-Navy-carrier-pilot reflexes didn't fail me, and I crossed my legs so quickly that he missed and fell hard on the floor on the seat of his pants.

You'd have thought he'd just had a root canal or a tetanus shot. He screamed and ran to his mother, sobbing, and pointing in my direction. "He hit me!" When his parents asked what happened, I calmly replied, "He fell! I didn't hit him. Besides, I'd never hit the head of a household!"

I knew it was time to depart when they put the little Emperor to bed by placing granola cookies on the stairs as enticements. And it worked. He ate his way up the stairs into his bedroom. "How are you going to motivate him to go to school?" I asked quietly. "Oh, I'm sure we'll come up with something," they laughed.

"Yes, but what if the neighborhood dogs eat what you put out?" I smiled. "He'll lose his way just like Hansel and Gretel!" They didn't laugh at that one but got up to open the front door and turn on the porch light for me so I could make a quick getaway in my car.

Every time I see a tantrum in a shopping mall or a disturbance in a school yard, I look for Bradford the Barbarian. But maybe he's made it into junior high by now. He'll probably be a loser who asks, "What can you do for me?" instead of a winner who asks, "What can I do for you?"

I really haven't been angry for about 17 years. During that time, no one has tried to physically harm me or someone close to me. I have learned to adapt to stress in life, and I reserve my fear or anger for imminently physically dangerous situations. I rarely, if ever, get upset with what people say, do or don't do, even if it inconveniences me. I've learned to not sweat the small stuff.

I teach a stress management seminar and a conflict resolution workshop on Turning the Serenity Prayer into a Way of Life. You're familiar with the Serenity Prayer, by Reinhold Niehbur: "God, grant me the serenity to accept the things I cannot change, the courage to change the things I can, and the wisdom to know the difference." It's a marvelous lesson on how to be proactive, instead of reactive.

Three Rules for Turning Stress into Success

1. Accept the unchangable. Everything that has happened in your life to this minute is history. The greatest waste of energy is in collecting grudges, getting even, harboring ill will, and thinking of revenge. Success is the only revenge. Go on with your life, forgive your trespassers, and succeed in spite of them. You will be fulfilled and happy. They will forever wonder how you went on to becove so successful without and in spite of them.

2. Change the changeable. What is changeable is your next thought and action, your response to difficult times and difficult people. You can only control your immediate thought and action. Since most of what we do is a reflex, subconcious habit, it is wise not to act on emotional impulse but to wait a moment until reason can compete with your emotions. By all means, read Daniel Goleman's book, *Emotional Intelligence*. It will tell you why we do what we do, when we know better.

3. Avoid the unacceptable. Go out of your way to get out of the way of potentially dangerous behaviors and environments. When people tailgate you on the freeway, change lanes. When they hit your rear-view mirror with their high-beam headlights, change lanes. When there are loud, obnixious people at the table next to yours in the restaurant, get a new table or change restaurants. Don't let others rain on your parade. Also, avoid behaviors that are potentially dangerous, especially those regarding health, personal safety, and financial speculation based on emotion.

● ● ●

We aren't responsible for what happens around us or for what others do or think. We're responsible only for how we choose to respond. That's what builds our character. The writer Joan Didion said it well: "Character—the willingness to accept responsibility for one's own life—is the source from which self-respect springs."

However, many women have a hard time feeling that they can take full responsibility for what happens to them. We've been brought up to be subservient, to place our wishes after those of our parents, husbands, and children. We live in a society where many people still consider us second-class citizens, despite all the rights and privileges granted us by law.

Lech Walesa, the former Polish political leader, said: "Women are to have fun with. In politics, I prefer not to see a woman. Instead of getting all worked up, they should stay as they are—like flowers." The actor Charles Bronson believes that "Women are not equal and never could be." G.A. Gaskell wrote that "The emotion-natured woman must be subject to the dictates of the reasoning mind of man, or truth, justice, equity, peace, mercy are all suppressed in the soul." And the Reverend Jerry Falwell said of feminists, "These women just need a man in the house. They need a man to tell them what time of day it is and lead them home."

It's hard to believe, but these men all voiced these antiquated ideas at the end of the 20th century! However, they're hardly unique in their estimation of the rights and abilities of women. They are simply representative of what men often feel, even when they aren't so honest about it.

Weeding Out the Negative Ideas

We're not suggesting you fall into the trap of placing the blame on men for all the problems women face.

Instead, we're suggesting that you acknowledge where some of our insecurities are rooted and weed them out. If you want to be an achiever, you can't listen to negative ideas. And don't allow anyone to keep you from your goals.

Shannon Lucid had trained with NASA's original class of women astronauts and is a brilliant scientist, the veteran of four previous space missions. In March 1996, at age 53, the American space shuttle Atlantis took her to a rendezvous with the Russian space station, Mir.

There she was to spend five months doing research alongside two male Russian astronauts. When the Russian general, Uri Glazkov, heard Shannon would be joining the team, he expressed his pleasure because she would bring a feminine touch to the project. As he said, "Women like to clean."

Male chauvinism, even in the late 90s, wasn't surprising to Shannon. The daughter of a Baptist minister, she was always interested in science. In eighth grade she wrote a paper on Robert Goddard, the father of rocketry. When she announced she was going to grow up to be a rocket scientist, her teacher scoffed, "Even if there was a job like that, you wouldn't be able to have it because you're a girl."

That didn't stop her. Shannon earned her pilot's license and flew her father to his tent meetings. Her father remembers she would have followed him to the pulpit, except Baptists wouldn't allow women to preach. Shannon says, "I had to become an astronaut to get closer to God than my father could." Shannon Lucid wasn't about to allow anyone's opinion to stand in the way of her dreams.

There's never any reason to be held back just because you're a woman—unless you allow it. Sometimes you might have to turn in a direction different from the one you originally planned, but it's the end result that matters. You know your extraordinary potential better than anyone else.

Bucking the System

Dr. Virginia Apgar is a good example of how to change course and still get where you're going. In the 1930s, she was one of the first women to graduate from Columbia University's medical school, and she wanted to be a surgeon. However, after two years she was still fighting rigid sexism that was preventing her from using her skills effectively.

She realized, as she put it, "Women won't go to a woman surgeon—only the Lord can answer that one." So she altered her course and switched to anesthesiology, developing the field from one comprised mostly of badly trained female nurses to a recognized, highly specialized medical discipline. She became director of anesthesiology at Columbia-Presbyterian Hospital and the first full professor of anesthesiology in history.

What's more important to us is that she deviated from her original design and created a new one. During her work in delivery rooms, she realized that many newborns were being lost because symptoms weren't being noticed and recorded after birth. In 1951, she introduced the Newborn Scoring System, which measures pulse, respiration, muscle tone, reflexes and skin color, and identifies correctable problems. The "Apgar Score" was quickly adopted in hospitals around the world, and the test she developed is responsible for saving the lives of countless infants.

Virginia Apgar could have spent her career bucking the system and trying to make headway in an area that wasn't ready to receive her skills. That would have led to frustration and a poor use of her talents. Instead, she took a different path to success.

Dr. Apgar provides a lesson for all of us. The talents that we have been given, however great or small, are like seeds.

Either we take the responsibility for them and plant them and nurture them in fertile areas—or they wither and die.

Oprah Winfrey says, "My philosophy is that not only are you responsible for your life, but doing the best at this moment puts you in the best place for the next moment."

If It Is to Be, It's Up to Me

That's our attitude as well. The responsibility for me is mine. During your 20-minute meditation, you might want to use the mantra: "If it is to be, it is up to me."

When you discover where you're going and what's driving you, you'll find you can make decisions quickly and easily. Have you ever noticed how successful people appear as if their minds are made up automatically? They don't hesitate. They don't waffle back and forth. They decide what's important to them, choose to have it, and then do whatever it takes to get it.

We've talked about the uniqueness of every human being. Part of that uniqueness comes from the individual abilities each of us was given at birth. You may be gifted with talent in writing, entertaining, organizing, sports, or a thousand other areas. Each of those talents is like money in the bank. It's up to you to discover what you're good at and then work with that special ability to better yourself and those around you.

Luck = Opportunity + Preparation

Carla Leeds is a talent agent in Los Angeles. She says, "Share your talents. Whether your specialty is baking, singing or painting, donate your time and talents to your community whenever you can. Someone of importance and influence just may notice, and you never know where that could lead."

We make our own luck, and by giving we can reap huge rewards. It's back to the idea—"what goes around, comes around."

Cynthia Brown found that out. From the time she was a little girl singing in church in Florida, people prophesied she'd be a singer. Her parents were urged to send her to New York for professional training, but the money just wasn't there. Instead, she attended the local community college and went to work as a secretary.

After she married and had three children, her dreams of an entertainment career faded even further, and she confined her singing to church on Sunday. She was 40 years old when a talent scout heard her at the Sunday service and signed her to sing at Universal Studios' theme park in Orlando. She performs there five times daily, sang the National Anthem at an NBA game, and has been sent on promotional trips across America and to London, Paris and Berlin—all this because she never stopped donating her voice to God on Sundays.

Many would say that Cynthia Brown was lucky. Poet Emily Dickinson summed up luck this way: "Luck is not chance, It's toil, Fortune's expensive smile, Is earned."

Lucille Ball said, "I don't know anything about luck. Luck to me is something else: hard work and realizing what is opportunity and what isn't."

The one definition that says it all is this: Luck happens when preparation meets opportunity.

An old joke warns you not to be at the railroad station "when your ship comes in." There's a good moral to that. Many of us are so busy wishing for something wonderful to happen that we never get around to getting ready for when it finally does.

Take Control of Your Mind and Body

We aren't victims of the winds of fate. We're standing at the helm, steering our own ships. We're not puppets, dangling from the strings of our heredity and environment. We have the ability to cut the strings that hold us back and to go out on our own. Responsible self-control, leading to self-discovery of our potential and preparation for our successes, is the path to mental health and frequently to physical health, as well.

Current research into bio-behavior and bio-feedback programs have verified the human potential for the control of body functions and brain wave emissions. We can even use relaxation techniques to reduce blood pressure. After specialized training and discipline, it's possible—and maybe even practical—for us to control our pulse rate, our threshold of pain, our brain wave frequencies and other body functions as a means of positive health maintenance for the future. We have much more voluntary control over what we thought were involuntary body functions than we ever imagined.

For example, today clinics throughout the world are teaching people how to raise their body temperature to help prevent the onset of a migraine headache. Patients learn how to dilate their arteries to permit greater blood flow to the heart, and how to relax muscles and nerve endings. Oncologists report that remissions and cures among cancer patients depend almost as much on the patients' attitude as on their medication.

The actress Helen Hayes, who was almost 90 when she died, put it this way: "Positive attitudes—optimism, high self-esteem, an outgoing nature, joyousness, and the ability to cope with stress—may be the most important bases for continued good health."

Limitations Are Self-Imposed

It's important that you don't leave the development of your potential to chance. Every day, thousands are finding that there's a bright new world out there, waiting to be discovered. And if we don't find it, it's because we've become victims of our negative habits—a prisoner of hundreds of restrictions of our own making.

Teenagers have a strong need to conform to the standards of their group. While they may feel that their special way of grooming is an act of independence, on the contrary, their styles and activities adhere very strictly to the peer group code. They have yet to realize that in their nonconformity, they are conforming.

Young people who refuse to be responsible for their own deeds, and who look to their peers for behavior cues, haven't yet reached responsible maturity. Unfortunately, many adults spend their entire lives at this same level of immaturity. They never discover that true adult freedom comes from accepting responsibility for our actions—and for our potential—instead of sidestepping it.

As we grow into adulthood, we make decisions that progressively narrow our opportunities and alternatives. We select only a few friends out of the hundreds of people we meet. Usually the friends we choose are people with whom we agree, which limits our intake of fresh ideas.

We choose our educational level. Some of us drop out of school at 16 or perhaps hang in, but only through high school graduation, instead of going on to college. Our education, in turn, determines to a great extent our jobs and our associates. From day to day, these people seek the path of least resistance, free from the hindrance of information or education or challenge—comfortable in their safe, established ways.

We call these individuals the security seekers. They pre-determine, to some extent, how far they will go in their careers. They form friendships and then close their circle of friends. They tend to seek out a comfort zone, preferring not to move unless they absolutely must. They abhor change, and when forced to change, they change as little as possible. When faced with a challenge or opportunity, they'll avoid it if possible. When confronted, they'll take the easy way out.

These no-risk security seekers rarely test their potential. They are seldom concerned about personal or career growth. They tend to see their career as a job and to define free time as a means of escaping from that job. They hate taking chances. They prefer not to know when something goes wrong. They may not know what it takes to succeed, but they usually know how to avoid failure.

● ● ●

Deborah: I clearly remember the exact day I made a conscious decision to change my life and start excelling. Sitting on a stool in a plexiglass booth giving tokens to kids and teens, I can still hear the clumps and clattering, the buzzes and bells of the Pinball Plus video arcade. This job was one of many I had held as I struggled to stay afloat after my divorce. Although it paid only $4.50 an hour, I could study my graduate homework and bring my 8-year old son to work with me. On this particular day, however, I had reached my breaking point. The starving student mentality wasn't working for me anymore.

I realized I had a bad case of PMS—Poverty Mentality Syndrome—a state of mind that kept me from excelling in life. I had thoughts such as "life is so tough," "I can barely make ends meet," "I can't seem to get ahead," and "things may not get any better," and they were shaping this rut I found myself in. I was determined to change my mind.

During my breaks I began opening my journal and taking inventory of my life, assessing my current situation. Describing exactly where I was in life and what I was doing, I took a hard look at my habits and behaviors that were not serving me. I made a list of affirmations to replace the negative self-talk that had become a normal part of my day. Right then and there, I made a solid commitment to myself, in writing, to break out of this rut, whatever it took.

I identified and listed some action steps I could take immediately to begin to change my life. The first was to step out of this easy and mindless job to secure a higher paying position, ideally a career. I searched the classifieds in several cities and inquired into the jobs that sparked my interest. Researching companies at the local library, I gathered information that would support my efforts. I targeted a Fortune 500 company in Houston, Texas, that was hiring consultants with a business or psychology background for a management development academy to be trained as internal change agents. I sought professional advice on my resume development and sent it off as a long shot.

One month later I relocated to Houston, Texas, leaving my $4.50 an hour job converting change into tokens—to a $45,000+ salary as a change agent converting status quo and resistance into a culture of continuous improvement. My self-determination helped me overcome my own resistance to the status quo in my life and catapulted me to a new level where I could develop, contribute, and excel.

P.S. Believe me, you men are just as susceptible to this form of PMS as we women are! It is easy to get caught in a rut of poverty mentality, especially when you begin to feel frustrated and helpless about being able to make changes in your life. "Taking action" is a male strong suit, and you have the potential to break out of your current circumstances when you realize your limitations are self-imposed. But remember, it is important that you practice the art of "going within" and "reflecting" as you decide to excel.

• • •

The Greatest Risk Is Doing Nothing

Total security is a myth. In fact it's one of the greatest myths you can ever believe, especially today in a downsized, outsourced, global village where the only rule is change.

Today you must be the CEO of your daily life: act self-employed, no matter who you work for; be completely responsible to remain employable, skilled, and healthy; and save for your own retirement. Depending on the government for your future financial security is like hiring an accountant who is a compulsive gambler!

Life is inherently risky. Driving is a risk. Flying is a risk. Entering a relationship is a risk. Beginning a new job is a risk. And starting your own business is a risk. The biggest risk is one you should avoid, however. That's the risk of doing nothing.

There Can Be No Freedom without Responsibility

Responsible achievers, on the other hand, become aware of the chains they've placed on themselves through their apathy and lack of imagination. After this moment of truth, they figure a way out of their predicament. They may go back to school and earn one or more degrees, continuing to study throughout their lives.

They opt for a career instead of just a job. They change their friends so they receive intellectual stimulation. In short, they assert their option to choose and assume their rightful role of personal responsibility for living up to their potential.

Famed anthropologist-sociologist, Margaret Mead, called "personal responsibility" the most important sign of our evolution. At the same time, she said the notion that we're the product of our environment is our biggest error.

In the same vein, historian Margaret Hamilton wrote, "When the freedom they wished for most was freedom from responsibility, then Athens ceased to be free and was never free again." The lack of responsibility brought down a proud city-state in ancient Greece. Don't let it be your undoing, as well.

Whether it's a government or a person, the concept remains the same. Without personal responsibility, there is no way that you can be in control of your own destiny.

• • •

Denis: For many years, I and the late Viktor Frankl, who wrote the classic human-purpose book, *Man's Search for Meaning*, petitioned our friends and colleagues to help us fund and erect a new statue of responsibility as the forgotten side of freedom. I briefly mentioned this in my book *Empires of the Mind* (1996) as I did in my first book, *The Psychology of Winning* (1978).

You can take a quantum leap in your own quest for excellence, financial freedom, and total fulfillment by understanding the full meaning of and embracing this critical concept of "The Statue of Responsibility." To do this, travel ahead with me in time to the year 2020, and as the year implies, get a clear vision of what could happen to our society if we equate our precious freedom of choice with freedom from responsibility.

Is the following imagined scenario a premonition of reality, or pure fantasy? You be the judge.

It is July 4, 2020. I, Denis Waitley, have turned 87 years of age less than one month ago. There are over 10 million other Americans my own age or older, so it's no big deal. I look forward to celebrating my 100th birthday in the year 2033, along with a quarter of a million other men and women in the United States.

We plan a satellite, video, big-screen celebration in the Superdome, Texas Stadium, and the Rose Bowl, where we can all do the "wave" in unison, if we can still stand up by then.

I remember, years ago, when reaching 100 was fairly rare. Now it is the fastest growing segment of the population.

In those days, Willard Scott of the old Today Show (which used to be on NBC, a major TV network, before the 1000 cable and Direct Digital PC and TV stations made the networks obsolete) would announce your name on national TV, and you'd maybe get a letter from the president of the United States. Today, in the year 2020, there are so many people celebrating their 100th birthday that you get a personal video phone call from the President, which rings on your PC, and she chats with you from her desk in the Oval Office on a video conference line serving 500 centenarians in a one-minute live greeting twice a week.

This July 4th, 2020, is a special one for me. It is the 244th anniversary of our American Independence Day, and I am taking four of my grandchildren and great grandchildren to visit the newly opened Statue of Responsibility monument in San Francisco. My grandson Jake, now 40, has two children in high school: Derek and Joy. My grandsons Shane and Alexander, now 29, each have a son, Matthew and Thomas, respectively, entering the first grade. My grandson Kyler is still single, traveling the globe by commercial space shuttle. My granddaughter Alissa, now 27 and still single, has just received her Ph.D. in psychoneuroimmunology from Shanghai-Stanford Medical School, which years ago was called Stanford University. Her cousin Danica, my youngest granddaughter, just cut a Digital Virtual Disk as a vocalist for the hottest new label, Net Rom.

Since Alissa graduated a few weeks ago, we decided to have our family reunion in the Bay Area and get all the great-grandkids together. I'm glad my wife, Susan, is younger than I am. At 87, having two teenage great-grandchildren and two seven-year-old great-grandsons jumping around the rickety old cable cars onto the magnetically-levitated moving outdoor escalators up and down the vertical San Francisco streets, puts my digital pacemaker into overdrive.

It seems like all these young kids want to do today is go to either the Jurassic Virtual Reality Themepark, where they can play hide and seek with the dinosaurs, or go to the Intergalactic Virtual Reality Themepark and have a laser fencing dual with cabbage-headed Klingons. I long for the good old days when you couldn't actually beam yourself inside the computer graphics and become part of the video game. I keep worrying about a power surge from an earth tremor that might trap my third generation offspring inside the game, and the only way we could see them again would be to project them onto the video screen built into the wall of our home. It may sound stupid to you, but it worries me. Can you imagine the movie version? Something like, "Honey, I digitized the kids?"

I know I sound a little "wired" and flippant in this story, but there's a somber side to this virtual reality trip.

As we board the huge Hydrofoil tour boat at Pier 39 for the 45-minute excursion around the magnificent new Statue of Responsibility, I sadly reflect on the last quarter of a century in America and wonder about the future for my great-grandchildren and their families.

Looking back at the San Francisco skyline and its gleaming buildings, against a backdrop of curling fingers of morning fog, I see the Sumitomo Center and Hong Kong

Bank Center that used to be the Transamerica and Bank of America buildings. I pick out the marquis of hotels that for decades served as proud San Francisco landmarks. I no longer see the Mark Hopkins, Sir Francis Drake, Fairmont, Hilton and Mansions Hotels. Instead I gaze at the new Peninsula, Shangri-La, Royal Garden, Mandarin Oriental and Miyako Hotels.

I remember from history about the Chinese who first arrived in San Francisco in the 1850s, and the merchants and laborers who helped plant the orchards and build the railroads of the west. I wonder if, as newly arrived immigrants in the 1800s, they ever dreamed their future offspring would convert Chinatown starting in Portsmouth Square, where the first tall ships docked, south on Grant Avenue from North Beach to the Financial District, into the most industrious and powerful society in America in a century and a half? Could they have seen what we Anglo-Americans were blind to envision as the preview of the future?

As the hydrofoil picks up speed and begins to plane smoothly above the choppy waves of San Francisco Bay, I look up at the majestic presence of the Statue of Responsibility as she faces the Golden Gate Bridge. She rises to a height of 310 feet from her pedestal base on Alcatraz Island, and at the top there is an eagle ready to take flight from her outstretched hand.

I remember another Lady in the harbor in the East, and what she represents. The Statue of Liberty, the symbol of American democracy and a beacon of refuge for immigrants, stands on Liberty Island in New York Harbor. France gave the Statue of Liberty to the United States in 1884 as a gesture of friendship and as a lasting reminder of the precious liberty that citizens enjoy under a free form of government.

As the tour boat docks at the Alcatraz wharf and my four great-grandchildren scramble ashore to explore the incredible new Statue of Responsibility, given to us by the Asian Common Market Countries, who now represent the dominant economic and social course of the 21st century, I feel that it is both ironic and yet somehow appropriate that this new historic statue stands here on Alcatraz, a rusting reminder of lost freedom, as a result of irresponsible choices and actions in a democratic society.

I hope, somehow, that my great-grandchildren get the message. I know my grandchildren have.

If you take the good things for granted, you must earn them again. For every right that you cherish, you have a duty which you must fulfill. For every hope that you entertain, you have a task you must perform. For every good that you wish to preserve, you will have to sacrifice your comfort and your ease. There is nothing for nothing in this world. Freedom has always carried a price of individual responsibility and the just rewards of your own choices.

The Statue of Responsibility has for many years been a cause and a vision of mine. I pray that if it is ever actually built, it will symbolize how we remembered, in time, the obligations of freedom, rather than symbolizing, too late, the lessons from our immigrant ancestors that we forgot.

Inscribed on my theoretical Statue of Responsibility, at the base of the pedestal on Alcatraz Island, I imagine these immortal words that were part of the family creed of industrialist-turned-philanthropist John D. Rockefeller, Jr. Those words he wrote a century ago are as alive and relevant today as they were when he coined them. They are ideally suited for the woman seeking independence:

> I believe in the supreme worth of the individual and in his of her right to life, liberty, and the pursuit of happiness. I believe that every right implies a responsibility; every opportunity an obligation; every possession a duty.

I believe that the law was made for people and not people for the law; that government is the servant of the people and not their master. I believe in the dignity of labor, whether with head or hand; the world owes no one a living, but it owes everyone an opportunity to make a living.

I believe that thrift is essential to well-ordered living and that economy is a prime requisite of a sound financial structure, whether in government, business, or personal affairs. I believe that truth and justice are fundamental to an enduring social order. I believe in the sacredness of a promise, that a person's word should be as good as his or her bond, that character—not wealth or power or position—is of supreme worth.

I believe that rendering useful service is the common duty of people and that only in the purifying fire of sacrifice is the dross of selfishness consumed and the greatness of the human soul set free.

I believe in an all-wise and all-loving God, and that the individual's highest fulfillment, greatest happiness, and widest usefulness are to be found in living in harmony with His will.

I believe that love is the greatest thing in the world; and that it alone can overcome hate; that right can and will triumph over might.

Self-Control Exercise

We want to give you some techniques for developing a winning attitude of positive self-control so that you can discover your potential and take responsibility for your actions.

1. Eliminate the verbs "I have to" and "I can't" from your vocabulary. Just get rid of them. They're false and misleading. Replace them with the determinate action verbs "I want to" and "I will."

2. Divide a page in your journal into two columns. On the left, write down a list of your current habits, especially those you don't much like. These can include things like wasting time in front of television, spending too much money, or not exercising enough.

94

On the right side of the page, write the alternative choices to those habits. Make them positive actions rather than negative. For instance, instead of smoking, you will breathe clean air. Instead of watching television the moment you get home or after you eat, you will take a walk. Instead of staying up late every night, you will get adequate rest.

3. Take the credit—and the blame—for your decisions openly. We want you especially to take the credit, because wherever you are, it's your choice to stay or leave. Even if your decision hinged on the advice of someone else, it was you who finally made it.

4. Affirm yourself with positive self-talk. Say, "My rewards in life will always match my service."

5. Be different, if it means higher personal and professional standards of behavior; if it means putting more time and effort into everything you do; and if it means taking calculated risks.

6. Be willing to take the heat of criticism and jealousy from people who would like to keep you stuck in place with them. The price of success is distancing yourself from a peer group that isn't helping you succeed and therefore tends to hold you back.

7. Control your memberships and your associations. You choose your role models, mentors, and friends. Network with people who are successful, who have similar goals and aspirations, and who have solved problems you may have, rather than those who share the same problem you have.

8. Learn how to relax and take more control of your body. Practice some deep relaxation methods. Study and learn more about bio-feedback techniques. Relax your muscles to get rid of tension. Learn how to relax and elevate your temperature to increase your blood flow and reduce your heart rate.

9. Set a specific time each week to initiate some action on your own behalf. Because the top achievers don't wait for an invitation to succeed, they make their own luck.

Make It Happen!

Losers let it happen. Achievers make it happen! So, in your journal, create your own positive forecast.

Self-determination is the success characteristic that makes you take responsibility for causing your own effects in life—and allows you to dare to choose to win.

You are three steps closer to where you want to go in life. In the next chapter, we will talk about self-motivation, which ignites the burning desire to succeed!

What Every Woman Needs to Know

Security provided by others is a myth. The only security is within oneself. We are all risk-managers in a world of constant change and uncertainty.

What Every Man Need to Understand

Being assertive is more comfortable and ingrained in men's psyche. As women assert themselves more in society, support them and nurture them as they make the uncomfortable transition. Also, understand and help them understand the difference between being assertive and being aggressive. Aggressiveness has caused most wars; assertiveness has resulted in progress for civilization.

Chapter 5

———•———

Desire from Within

Discover your potential, deserve to win, dare to choose—and now we invite you to take the next step: cultivate the desire that provides inner fire. Desire hinges on the achiever's action quality of positive motivation.

•   •   •

Denis: Self-motivation is the inner drive that puts belief into action for winning in life. The main theme of this important characteristic is the knowledge that winners are driven by desire from within. I can't think of a consistent winner in any walk of life who didn't first internalize that burning desire to succeed. Winners know the basic behavioral axiom in life, which Earl Nightingale first introduced to millions of listeners as "The Strangest Secret": You and I "become what we think about most."

In other words, every day you and I are motivated and moved by what we are thinking about most. What our minds are dwelling on determines the direction we take and the choices we make. Everything we do in life is self-motivated, either a little or a lot, and either positively or negatively. Even if you decide to do nothing, it's a decision based on motivation.

•   •   •

The Inner Fire

The word "motivation" is derived from the word "motive." If you look up the definition of "motive," you'll find it's defined as that within the individual, rather than outside, which excites him or her to action.

Everything we do is done for a specific motive. When we eat, our motive is to relieve hunger. When we sleep, our motive is to rest the body. When we go to a movie, our motive is to be entertained.

Even when we stop at a red light, complete an assignment at work or walk along the beach collecting shells, there is some motive behind what we do.

"Motivation" is a strong tendency toward or away from an object or situation. The good news is, motivation can be learned and developed. It isn't inborn.

A force that compels behavior is most powerful and lasting when it comes from within. You know where you're going because you have a compelling image inside, not because of a full-page magazine ad, television commercial, or pep talk from your boss. The performance of many externally motivated people begins declining as soon as they reach some level of material achievement.

If you're really committed to peak performance and leadership, you must motivate yourself—and those who look to you for guidance—from within. Studies of achievers show that inner drives for excellence and independence are far more powerful than desire for wealth, status, or recognition.

Behavioral scientists have found that independent desire for excellence is the most telling predictor of significant achievement. In other words, the success of our efforts depends less on the efforts themselves than on our motives. The most successful companies, like the most successful men and women in almost all fields, have achieved their greatness out of a desire to express what they felt had to be expressed. Often it was a desire to use their creative abilities to their utmost in order to solve a problem or fill a need. Of course, many of them have also earned a great deal of money and notoriety for their efforts.

Pursue Your Passion

Coco Chanel, Esteé Lauder, Mary Kay Ash, Gloria Estefan, Danielle Steele, and Oprah Winfrey all became wealthy. But far more than thoughts of profit, the real key to their success was inspiration and inner drive by creating or providing excellence in a product or a service. All were self-motivated by the desire to produce the very best, to express the very best that was in them.

Desire from within is the difference between getting a job to earn a paycheck and being engaged in an exciting career. A job is a necessary interruption between weekends. But a career is something you do because you want to do it, you love doing it, you're excited when you do it, and you'd do it even if you were paid only enough for basic sustenance. You'd do it because it's your life.

Finding this passion, this inner fire of desire, will make you oblivious to watching the clock and worrying about the length of your workday. You'll awaken without needing an alarm clock to jar you out of bed, and you'll face the day with the passion of pursuit, but not necessarily the pursuit of money. Those who are inspired and passionate about their contributions, who do more than is asked of them, are always sought for their services and, although that wasn't their primary motive, their name and work outlive them and always command the highest salaries and pay.

Loving your career is especially important for younger people. If you compromise yourself at an early age by taking a job solely for the pay, you may be working primarily for money all your life. If you lose the passion for what you are doing early, you may never grow to anywhere near your potential for self-actualization.

Fear: The Great Inner Compeller

Like the inner fire of desire, fear is also a powerful motivator. Just as you are propelled by desire, you can be compelled by fear. We all know of individuals, both in professional and personal life, who resort to threats, power plays and punishment in the mistaken idea that it's the fastest way to the top of the mountain. In the short run, fear forces you to comply or else. In the long run, its effect is to stagnate or paralyze the will to achieve.

Fear is ever-present in all of our lives. By understanding what causes our fears, we can learn how to deal with them. When you're afraid, you're always looking backward over your shoulder, worried about what's sneaking up on you from behind.

The fear of physical danger is an automatic instinct. This fear causes us to react to what we perceive as life-threatening, with the fight or flight response.

Unfortunately, most of us tend to have this knee-jerk reaction to every daily confrontation, flaring to anger quickly and becoming defensive in situations that call for calmness and reason.

Since many women have a more spontaneous ability to express emotions such as passion, they are motivated from within more readily than most men, who seem to thrive more on competition and going for an external prize. Conversely, women also may express more instinctive reactions to that which they perceive as personally threatening. The best way to overcome this built-in fear of danger is knowledge. Get the facts of the situation and act accordingly. Fear dissipates and often disappears with knowledge and action.

A second fear is the fear of success, which isn't recognized by most people. It is disguised as guilt when we experience something we consider "too good to be true" for our own self-concept. Working on self-acceptance and self-confidence by gaining knowledge, skills and experience also overcomes this fear.

Finally, the greatest fear we have to face in life is the fear of failure, which is really a fear of rejection. We all have a natural aversion to being embarrassed or made a fool of in the presence of others. More than any other motivating factor, this fear of what might happen holds us back and causes us to procrastinate. We permit ourselves to be motivated by inhibition or the fear of failure—rather than moved forward by the ignition of the fire of our inner desires. That's why being able to work through disappointments and handle failures is so vitally important to the self-motivation of high achievers.

● ● ●

Deborah: A huge fear for me in my life, as I think it is to some degree in all of us, is the fear of the unknown. Death is at the farthest end of the scale, yet even a potentially positive transition such as leaving a secure job to pursue a passion can also provoke fear. It is human nature to seek security, one of our fundamental needs. Any change or threat to the "known" in our lives can be frightening.

I'd had an illustrious career at the Fortune 500 company, starting as a separate consultant, then promoted to corporate trainer, then again promoted to an executive position managing MBA-level consultants. Early mornings I stood at my window on the 35th floor of the corporate tower and watched the sun illuminate the Houston skyline. Late at night I walked to my car through the balmy air of the bayous to the hypnotic sound of the cicadas.

Being female was especially challenging in the "good-old-boy" culture, and I battled the resistance to change by working harder and smarter. Designing, facilitating, and directing strategic improvement initiatives, I knew I was making a significant contribution by bringing a creative and humanistic approach to the bottomline objectives of the company.

Years had passed, and I began to sense the longings of an unfulfilled part of myself. I knew there was more to learn and explore, and I became keenly interested in the field of transpersonal psychology, a discipline that combines clinical psychology, eastern philosophy, and self-actualization. Much to the chagrin of my family and friends, I left the security of my career to pursue doctoral studies in an area that fueled my passion.

Some called it risky, others labeled it crazy—I called it a leap of faith. How many of you have felt that deep burning within when you want something so badly, you don't worry whether there will be a net to catch you if you fall? You know that somehow you will land safely.

I joined a nutritional network marketing company to support myself through school. Within eight months, I was earning the same amount of money as my corporate job, yet working only part-time—and pursuing my passion. And I was now enjoying better health than I had been in the last 15 years. The fuel of self-motivation ignited the fire of success and fulfillment.

P.S. I know that for most men a leap of faith such as this can have greater risks. If you are the primary breadwinner of your family and have children depending on you for their financial needs, including college education, it is easier said than done. Often, women are in a better position to make these kinds of moves. I suggest that you begin by listening to your inner desires, perhaps developing them into part-time hobbies at first, and then maintain a healthy balance between your passion and your responsibilities.

• • •

Failure Is Fertilizer

The best way to conquer the fear of failure is to redefine the term and your understanding of it. View mistakes as corrective feedback to get you back on track. High achievers are willing to accept a certain amount of failure in their lives. They aren't afraid of it and it doesn't destroy their self-motivation when they experience it. Failure and mistakes are the dues we pay to understand the value of our successes.

So in the psychology of winning for women there are no mistakes or failures, only lessons. Growth is a process of gaining knowledge, of trial and error, and of courageous experimentation. The failed attempts can be as much a part of the success process as the attempt that finally succeeds.

• • •

Denis: One of my mentors, the late Dr. Jonas Salk, who developed the first effective polio vaccine, told me that he devoted 98 percent of his time to documenting things that didn't work in his pursuit of things that did.

Just as guilt can be tied deeply to the belief that we don't deserve success, so are guilt and rejection tied deeply to failure. The experience of a failure, which results in feelings of disappointment, is actually like being told to go to your room or stand in a corner because you've been a naughty girl.

People equate failure with the worst of punishments, which is the fear of peer rejection or a loved one's disapproval.

We know of hundreds of individuals who come out of the ghetto to greatness and come out of bankruptcy back to success, but the emotional injuries seem to be the most difficult to heal. To succeed, you've got to look at failures as temporary inconveniences and fertilizer to grow on.

Desire stimulates the positive motivation, overrides the fear, and urges you forward. Desire makes you concentrate on the results of success rather than on the possible problems. When you desire your dream with burning intensity, you dwell on the rewards of success and not the penalties of failure.

Whether you're an executive, educator, doctor, nurse, athlete or homemaker, desire makes you respond positively to the pressures in your life.

• • •

Ayn Rand, the author of *Atlas Shrugged* and *The Fountainhead*, said, "People create their own questions because they're afraid to look straight. All you have to do is look straight and see the road, and when you see it, don't sit looking at it—walk."

That's good advice, but it's not always feasible. If you think about the reward at the end of the road, it's easy to move toward what you want. If you concentrate on the penalty, however, you tend to move toward the penalty and away from the reward. A penalty of failure is a very real goal. Unfortunately, it's like a car going in reverse toward the bumper of the car following behind.

Here's an illustration of what we're talking about. Say you put a $20 bill at one end of a wooden plank and ask a friend if she would walk on the plank to pick up the money. Of course she would; it's easy money.

Then, once she's agreed, take her up to the top of a five-story building, set one end of the plank on the edge of the roof, and set the other end, with the $20 bill secured to it with a rubber band, on the edge of the roof next door. Now ask your friend if she is still willing to walk that plank to get the money.

Of course she won't be willing, because $20 isn't worth the danger of falling and getting killed. Maybe for $1 million, but not for $20. The negative tension created by the penalty of falling makes the goal of the reward invisible because of the fear of the street below.

Negative Thoughts = Negative Results

Another aspect of motivation and desire is that the mind responds to what it hears. If you tell your kids, "Your room is a pigsty—it's never going to be clean!" you can be sure that the room will remain in danger of being condemned by the Board of Health. You've set up a negative image, and you're going to get a negative response. It's like motivating an office staff by saying, "Firings will continue until morale improves." It'll never work.

• • •

Dayna: My sister Deborah is not just a sibling to me, she is my best friend. I'm sure she won't mind if I share one of her more challenging and enlightening teenage experiences with you. It was an event that demonstrated to our entire family, especially our dad, how negative thoughts reap negative results.

One Sunday afternoon I heard my dad announce to Deborah, "I'm going to run some errands now, so whatever you do, don't take the keys to the new car. It's too powerful, and you just got your driver's license. Whatever you do, don't take that car for a drive! Any questions on what I don't want you to do?"

She shook her head sheepishly and replied, "No questions at all, Dad."

At that time he did not fully appreciate how dominant thoughts equal dominant behavior or how difficult it is to motivate someone by the reverse of an idea.

He then drove off in our old blue station wagon, leaving the brand new 240Z sports car beckoning in the driveway.

Within fifteen minutes, Deborah bounced into my room with a gleam of adventure in her eye. "Come on, Dayna," she coaxed. "Let's take that new car on a little test drive—just for a minute—just for a second! It must be really great if Dad doesn't want us to take it!"

For a moment, I imagined the thrill of two teenagers venturing out on the open road. Then my excitement gave way to anxiety, and I declined my sister's risky enticement.

An hour later I learned that Deborah's seemingly harmless adventure had gone terribly wrong. Deborah had driven the car to the center of town to see the new Halloween window paintings that decorated the local shops. She backed into a parking space. She put the car in park, marked "R," then stepped on the accelerator to rev up the engine—and catapulted through the largest department store in our hometown!

Fortunately, the store was closed. She drove through women's lingerie, men's wear, and jewelry. She totaled the car and totaled the store, but, miraculously, no one was hurt. The only thing Deborah broke was her pride.

Later that evening, Deborah and Dad discussed the event in her bedroom. Although Deborah was still physically and emotionally shaken, she was ready to receive her expected tongue lashing.

In a trembling voice she sighed, "Dad, you must be furious with me."

To her relief and amazement he calmly replied, "Heck no, honey. I'm glad you are alive. I'm glad no one was hurt. No problem."

Deborah, caught a little off-guard, questioned, "No problem? Boy, that's how I like my dad—understanding! But what did I learn from this?"

Dad paradoxically responded, "You learned about motivation and responsibility."

Deborah interrupted, "Responsibility? Gosh, no, I was irresponsible!"

Dad sternly explained, "No, you were responsible. You see, I just talked to the storeowner, and he's given you a job starting tomorrow. $200 dollars a month for seven years."

Deborah's eyes widened in disbelief as she contemplated her seven-year sentence.

Dad continued, "By then, most of the store will be paid off, so will the car, and you will be able to buy your own car, knowing how to make monthly payments religiously."

Deborah then curiously inquired, "What did you learn from this, Dad?"

With a half-smile and a knowing look, he replied, "I have learned how to take the car keys with me, and how dominant thoughts equal dominant behavior."

• • •

The only good time to use fear motivation is when there's a chance of physical danger. "Don't run in the street or you'll get hit by a car." "Don't touch the flame or you'll get burned." "Don't take things from strangers or you could be hurt." If health and safety are in danger, that's when you use fear to stop unhealthy behavior or prod someone to run for cover.

Modified fear motivation can also work successfully when you've tried every other incentive to spark desire motivation without getting positive forward movement.

For example, you've used every way you know to get your teenager to do chores. Your last resort is to sit down and say, "I'm giving you one week to improve, which I know you can do. You are perfectly capable of helping out. At the end of the week, unless you meet the targets we've set, you'll not be allowed to go out with your friends on the weekends. If that isn't enough, we will begin taking away other privileges." You've given boundaries, a specific set of expectations, and added the fear motivation of being stuck in the house instead of doing what the child wants.

A word of caution: Don't withhold meals or activities that, deprived of, would seriously damage their self-esteem, such as not being able to appear in a school play, athletic event or musical. Remove privileges, not self-confidence-building activities.

Remember: Fear can stop bad behavior, but fear doesn't motivate people when you're trying to encourage positive behavior. It's like putting a gun to someone's head and saying, "Relax. Keep on doing your best and nobody will get hurt."

Dominant Thoughts = Dominant Behavior

Achievers know that what they think controls what they do. You can't tell your subconscious not to do something and expect it to obey. For example, try this: "Don't think about flying pink elephants!" Now, describe the first image that came to your mind. We would not be surprised if you saw a slew of winged pachyderms in pink.

Your subconscious mind has to be fed the positive information it needs to activate your progress toward your goal. That's why all affirmations have to be stated in positive rather than negative language. That's why you can't lose weight if you keep thinking about how fat you are. That's why you can't stop smoking if you keep telling yourself to put out the cigarette. And that's why you can't get rich if you think and act poor. What we feed into our subconscious is what life will feed back to us.

Research conducted by Carl Pribram, former head of neuropsychology at Stanford University, confirmed that the subconscious—which houses our long-term memory, habits and reactions—deals only with present-tense information. Since it has the responsibility of keeping our heart beating and our body functions working in the present moment, it doesn't deal with past or present information as history. It deals with all thoughts and actions as if they were happening right now, in the present tense.

Grace Speare explains it this way: "We must realize that the subconscious mind is the law of action and always expresses what the conscious mind has impressed on it. What we regularly entertain in our minds creates a conception of self. What we conceive ourselves to be, we become."

The danger inherent in turning your thoughts toward what you want is in deciding what you'll think about. The late pioneer of positive thinking—Norman Vincent Peale—liked to quote a road sign in upstate New York which read: "Choose your rut carefully. You'll be in it for the next 10 miles." If you choose to think dreary, discouraging thoughts, your wheels will be traveling deep in that rut, and it'll be harder and harder to climb out and get back in the fast lane. Your choice determines the next several miles, and possibly years, of your future.

Be Proactive, Not Reactive

Achievers see risk as opportunity. They can see the rewards of success before they reach them, and they don't fear the penalties of failure. This is fortunate because when you're dominated by fear, you can't act with choice or positive intent. You go through life reactive, defensive and incapacitated—instead of proactive, assertive, and strong.

Opportunities Missed
(or The Curse of Permanent Potential)

There was a very cautious woman
She rarely laughed, she rarely cried
She rarely risked, she hardly tried
She rarely sang, she rarely played
She rarely dreamed, she rarely prayed
And when she one day passed away
Her insurance was denied
For since she never really lived
They claimed she never died.

Proactive people don't wait for a situation to happen—they make the first move. They don't object to someone else's idea—they put their idea on the table first. They are eager and enthusiastic. They have dreams and goals and desires. Each new day brings fresh challenges and new rewards.

As Susan Polis Schutz wrote: "If you have a goal in life that requires a lot of energy, that incurs a great deal of interest and that is a challenge to you, you will always look forward to waking up to see what the new day brings."

And Florence Scovill Shinn, one of the early positive thinking writers, said: "You will be a failure until you impress the subconscious with the conviction that you are a success." She suggested that this happens best when you find the affirmation that "clicks" for you—the word or phrase that will kick your desire into high gear.

You'll find that people who are dominated by stress are unable to change the world they live in. Instead, they allow the world to alter them. They feel there's no point in dreaming great dreams because they will never be able to work up the desire to achieve them. Women, especially, are afraid to take the giant steps. We tend to hang back and give up on what we really want to have and do.

Sheila Graham wasn't that kind of woman. A feisty newspaper gossip columnist and the beloved companion of F. Scott Fitzgerald, she admonished that, "You can have anything you want if you want it desperately enough. You must want it with an exuberance that erupts through the skin and joins the energy that created the world."

Life Is What You Make It

If you knew Heidi Von Beltz, you'd see that kind of energy and exuberance—under conditions most of us can only dream of in nightmares.

Heidi was well on her way to the top as a movie stunt woman. Full of energy and determination, she was a six-foot tall teenager who excelled in sports. By the time she was in her mid-teens, she was a ski instructor as well as an expert rider and tennis player. She had a wonderful life, glamorous and exciting. Her friends were Hollywood stars, and she was getting parts in movies as a stunt woman so she could learn the business. Someday she would direct a major film. She was sure of it.

By the time she was 24, she had several film credits on her resumé and a zest for living that was unusual, even in show business. Then in 1980, an easy car stunt went horribly wrong on the set of the film *Cannonball Run*.

Heidi was paralyzed from her earlobes down. Her spinal cord was fractured, and several vertebrae in her neck were smashed. The doctors said she might live five years, but she'd certainly never walk again.

Heidi and her parents refused to accept the medical prognosis. She left the hospital, bought a house, and outfitted a gym with the money she received from the film's producers. She immediately began a grueling regimen of physical and emotional rehabilitation. Eight hours a day she worked on muscle-building and read books by positive thinking philosophers. Within the first year, she began to feel the stirrings of sensation in her legs and arms.

Eight years later she was able to sit up on her own. In 1995 she was fitted with lightweight aluminum leg braces and taught herself how to stand. Her goal was to be walking again in two years.

In her book, My Soul Purpose: Living, Learning and Healing, she says, "I've never been wrong in my goals." And she adds, "The notion that we're in control is such a difficult thing to grasp. You're a product of your imagination."

Heidi Von Beltz has far exceeded even the most optimistic prognosis. One doctor said, "Hers is not a medical recovery. It is a positive-attitude recovery."

Medical science admits that doctors can't heal people who don't want to be healed. They have a little more trouble accepting that even terminal patients can possibly turn their lives around and make a recovery. What is needed is a dream to latch onto firmly and the inner fire of deep desire to make it come true.

The writer Natalie Goldberg put it all into perspective for every woman when she wrote: "Life is not orderly. No matter how we try to make life so, right in the middle of it we die, lose a leg, fall in love, drop a jar of applesauce." The point is, it's not what life does to you—we all face challenges of one degree or another—the important thing is what you do with the life you were given. We have always believed, "Life is what you make it. It's not what happens that counts so much—it's how you take it!"

The Courage to Win

Alice Walker, who wrote *The Color Purple*, said, "Women have to summon up courage to fulfill dormant dreams." And Winifred Gordon said, "Many women miss their greatest chance of happiness through a want of courage in the decisive moments of their lives."

In the Atlanta Olympics, we saw that kind of courage at a decisive moment. Gymnast Kerri Strug, her leg badly injured, had to decide whether to drop out and let her team lose the gold medal, or take the plunge and risk further injury. As the world watched, Keri made the last vault, falling to her knees in agony a split second after nailing her successful landing.

She was carried to the winner's stand, and she was forced to sit on the sidelines during the individual events. But she showed the courage every one of us would wish to have at a decisive moment. She was motivated by an intense desire to make her dream come true, and her decision made her more famous than she had ever imagined.

Heidi Von Beltz and Kerri Strug are both athletes. They're movement-oriented, and that could account for much of their fierce determination. It's been proven that inactivity breeds despondency. It brings forth dark imaginings and distorts situations all out of proportion to reality. Without physical and mental activity, fear begins to beg for attention.

When We Get Busy, Things Tend to Regain Their Proper Perspective

After decades of interviewing, researching and studying the habits of high achievers, we know they have a correspondingly high degree of self-motivation.

113

This enduring power comes from inside and moves us to action. It's the source of our self-confidence, which allows us to desire our dreams so fervently that we know we'll achieve them.

Success in life isn't reserved for the talented, it's not dependent on a high IQ, and it's not always the result of superior skills or having the best equipment. Success is almost totally dependent on your inner drive—the extra energy required to make another effort, to try another approach, to gain more knowledge. That's the secret of winning.

We hope you are keeping your journal. Don't let a day go by without making some entry that has special meaning to you. Chart your progress as you develop into a positive achiever.

Motivation is best maintained with regular progress reports and a stair-step approach to goals, gaining reinforcement for small successes that turn into major accomplishments.

Self-Motivation in Action

We're going to give you some action reminders because we need to remember how to develop this winning action quality of self-motivation to keep the inner fires of desire burning intensely.

1. In your daily speech, make a conscious effort to replace "I can't" with "I can" and "I'll try" with "I will!" You'll find that "I can" applies to about 95 percent of the challenges you encounter every day. These simple semantic changes will establish your new positive attitude, dwelling on things you can do and will do.

2. Remember: "We become what we think about." Focus all your attention and energy on the achievement of the objectives you are involved in right now.

114

3. Forget about the consequences of failure. Failure is only a temporary change of direction to set you straight for your next success. The psychologist Dr. Joyce Brothers echoed that thought when she wrote, "The person interested in success has to learn to view failure as a healthy, inevitable part of the process of getting to the top."

So make a pact with yourself. We suggest you write an agreement with yourself in your journal. Promise that you won't allow a failure to be more than a learning experience that allows you to move more quickly to the place you want to be.

4. To stay self-motivated, keep your self-talk affirmative. Whether you're at work, at home or on the tennis court, your subconscious is recording every word. Instead of "I can't" say "I can. Instead of "should have" say "will do." Instead of "if only" say "next time." Instead of "Yes, but" say "Why not?" Instead of "problem" say "opportunity." Instead of "difficult" say "challenging." Instead of "I'll try" say "I will." Instead of "could have" say "My goal." Instead of "Someday" say "Today."

5. Forget perfection. Only the saints are perfect—and as the English writer Paula Hansford Johnson wrote, "Sainthood is acceptable only in saints." Accept the flaws and the failures in yourself, and consider them challenges and learning experiences. They are seeds of growth.

6. Declare a moratorium on negatives—negative thoughts, negative people, negative forms of entertainment. Keep your desire to succeed strong by erasing thoughts of the downside.

7. Make a list of five of your most important wants or desires. Then right next to each, write down the benefit or payoff when you achieve it. For instance, say you want to exercise more. Write that down, and next to it you might write: "Improve lean body mass and cardiovascular fitness."

Reread this list before you go to bed each night and each morning when you get up. It will be even more powerful if you read it aloud or write it over and over again.

Whatever you do, never allow your goals and their benefits to you to get lost in the back of your subconscious. Bring them out in the sunlight and shine them every day—and there's no way you can fail.

What Women Need to Know and Men Need to Understand

We all might adopt one of the classic mottos of the industrialist Henry Ford: "Whether you think you can or think you can't—either way you're right!"

Chapter 6

———●———

Dare to Believe

In this chapter, we explore the power of expectation. You are motivated only when you believe you will be able to accomplish what you set out to do. If you have the inner fire of desire and set out to cross a desert in search of a beautiful, lush oasis, how far would you get if you believed it was only a mirage? Motivation is directly proportional to the expected level of success.

● ● ●

Denis: Belief is the key to unlocking the door of success for every human being. Or it is the lock that imprisons and keeps that human being from ever experiencing success. As a positive power, belief is promise that future goals will be realized. As a negative power, it is the premonition of our deepest fears and despairs. There is an inextricable relationship between the spirit and the mind, as there is between the mind and the body. What is believed internally will be manifested externally in some way. Self-expectation is understanding the awesome force of the self-fulfilling prophecy. You may not get what you want in life, but you probably will get what you expect deep down in your core beliefs.

● ● ●

We have heard that all our lives. And we believe it. But we as women also realize that the quality of our expectations is the crucial issue.

117

We sometimes forget how powerful our minds really are. How we think is often a self-fulfilling prophecy. Our minds control us more than we are probably aware.

A nurse tells about a patient who was sent to a hospice by mistake. The laboratory had made an error, and the woman was told she was going to die, even though she was in no real medical danger. After a couple of days, the error was discovered, but the patient's condition continued to deteriorate. No matter how much reassurance she was given, because she believed she was going to die her body responded, slowly shutting itself down. Finally, the doctors and psychiatrists brought in the lab technician who had made the error to talk to the patient. Only then was she convinced she was going to be fine. It was a life-and-death struggle to reverse her mindset and begin her journey back toward health.

That's the tremendous power of the mind. Think about it. If your brain can allow you to die, it can also prevent you from living to the fullest. When you expect the worst, your expectations will be realized. You can count on it.

If you're like us, you enjoy reading about special women who accomplish things, women who have managed to overcome incredible odds to emerge victorious over the challenges in their lives. When you read these inspirational stories, do you ever feel that you're also a special person? Do you ever think about what you've done to make you stand out? Maybe you lobbied to have a stoplight installed at a busy intersection and saved lives in the process.

In the early 19th century, Hannah Stater revolutionized the textile industry. Her husband owned a textile mill in Rhode Island, and Hannah knew firsthand the problems of having flax thread break. She introduced sturdier cotton thread, and although you've never heard her name, she profoundly influenced an industry. Hardly a day goes by that we don't benefit from her invention.

Success Must Be Shared

Most successful people are so busy doing what they do—contributing in one way or another—that they never think of seeking publicity on their own. Usually it's left to someone else to bring them to our attention.

In the summer of 1996 the Tweeds clothing catalog, which mails 20 million catalogs a year, began a new campaign called "Women Giving Back." On their catalog covers, Tweeds features women who, in the company's words, "have achieved something significant" and who "are personally helping others."

The first cover had a picture of actress Molly Ringwald, with a two-page spread inside highlighting the work she does with her favorite charities.

Later, the cover role model was four-time Olympic gold medalist swimmer Janet Evans. Another nice aspect of the campaign is that all celebrity modeling fees are donated to the featured charities.

Now, you and I may never be on the cover of a catalog or a magazine or featured on radio or television, but does that mean we don't deserve it? Of course not. It just means we're not as visible as the celebrities who are chosen.

True success is internal. It reflects how well you devote yourself to doing the best for others—how well you use the talents you are given, the education you receive and the skills you learn. It's the outward manifestation of how well you develop your own internal standards and then live by them.

Live by Design, Not by Default

Two sets of expectations have a profound effect on how we design our lives. The first is the expectation others have

119

for us. The second—and more important—is the expectation we have for ourselves. Today more than ever before, women are realizing they don't have to live the existence planned for them.

Diane is a 50-something-year-old insurance executive. After a painfully short marriage in her early twenties, she did as she was expected to do. She returned home to live with her parents, remaining there to help them through their final years. In two years, she'll retire after 35 years with the company. Her widowed father is nearing 90, and so her job at home is almost over. And when you would expect her to sit back and collect her pension, what does she plan? No rocking chair, that's for sure. She says, "All my life I did what was expected of me. When my responsibility is over, I'm heading for M.I.T. in Boston to study naval architecture. I may never get to build a ship, but I'm going to know how—and have fun learning!"

In the same way, women who were directed toward nursing are going back to school to become doctors, bookkeepers are getting their C.P.A. certifications, and secretaries are becoming CEOs.

As the saying goes, "We're gonna fly from our cocoon and plant our footsteps on the moon, and on our way to chart the stars, we'll stop and check for life on Mars." We've only just begun our metamorphosis.

• • •

Denis: Just as it's destructive to allow others' expectations to design our lives, it's stunting to our personal growth when we shackle ourselves with our own low expectations. We have trouble expecting much because we feel we don't deserve much, and what the mind believes, the body acts on.

We hear the word "psychosomatic" all the time, but have you ever taken a minute and thought about what it really means? "Psycho" is "mind" in Greek, and "soma" is body. A psychosomatic illness is one in which the mind sickens the body without *any other illness present.* It can be just as ravaging as a real medical condition, and harder to cure because the culprit is a negative imagination that convinces the body it's sick.

Patients with psychosomatic disturbances are great examples of negative self-expectancy. They expect to be sick, and they are. They expect to have a bad day, and they do. They expect to be passed over for a raise—and they are.

Successful people expect the best to happen—and if it doesn't happen this time, they expect it will the next, or the next, or the next. They never give up. They know they deserve to get their piece of the pie, and they keep plugging along until they get it.

· · ·

Roberta Williams is the chief game designer for the computer games company, Sierra On-Line, which she and her husband recently sold for one billion dollars. Her field is dominated by men, and Roberta would be the first to admit she never felt she fit in. She had passed on going to college, married at 19, had a baby at 20, and at 25 was a bored and disillusioned housewife.

That's when her husband, Ken, a computer programmer, brought home a computer game. In no time, Roberta was hooked. She kept nagging Ken to start their own company because she wanted to develop new games more palatable to women as well as men. That meant games designed around adult fairy tales instead of shoot'em, bomb'em, destroy'em scenarios.

They shipped their first game in 1979. By the late 1990's, Roberta had invented 23 separate games, some of them ranking among the most popular in the world, and they had sold millions of copies. She says, "I felt deep down inside I'd do something really extraordinary or different." Her self-expectation was high. Her life design was on target. And her success was assured because of her own self-expectations.

Live Up to Your Own Internal Standards

Let's not lose sight of the point about the influence of expectations on the design we draw for our lives. While our personal expectations are vital, the expectations that others place on us can be a limiting factor for many women.

If you're over 35, you may have had some flack from your family because you wanted a career. Maybe you chose to postpone marriage and children. Perhaps you preferred to be single, but the guilt laid on by well-meaning parents made you reconsider.

A very well-known speaker, a woman who talks to corporate America from one coast to the other, has carved out a wonderful life for herself without a husband or children. She's in her forties, lives a busy life from a delightful home, has tons of dates, time for friends of both genders, and has no eyes to ever marry.

Does she like men? She'll tell you she "adores" them, spends time with them, counts them as close friends and confidants, but she doesn't marry them. She expected her life to go in another direction.

Many women, on the other hand, manage to combine the whole package with flair—kids, husband, home, and career.

And that's the point. It doesn't matter what anyone else expects. It doesn't matter what society dictates. It doesn't matter what our mothers or grandmothers did. Each of us has to make her own decision about what's going to work best in her life—and then go for it.

• • •

Dayna: What is so exciting about the new millennium for women is that we have so many choices! You can find happiness in your own back yard—and the world is your oyster, too! You can pursue an exciting and meaningful career or enjoy the noblest profession, motherhood.

The stay-at-home mom does not need to apologize or rationalize to anyone about her decision to raise her children full-time. Ignore the media images that glorify the working woman and make some full-time mothers feel like third-class citizens. Many career women have decided to step out of the work arena and channel all their efforts into their families.

The first playgroup I ever attended with my two-year-old daughter, Alissa, heightened my awareness of some of the insecurities that some women harbor about motherhood. Like most playgroups it was a wonderful opportunity for full-time mothers and toddlers to converge and socialize. At the first meeting, however, I was quite surprised when one of the mothers introduced herself with a bit of sarcasm saying, "Hi, I'm Lisa Richards, and I used to be an attorney. What did you used to be?"

She assumed that when a woman opts for full-time motherhood she negates all that she has accomplished or aspired to in the past. I was quick to put her comment in proper perspective by replying, "Well, I am a psychologist on sabbatical as a full-time mom." I tried to make her feel more valued by sharing a few of my favorite quotes: "It is better to have the respect of one child than the adulation of many" and "The hand that rocks the cradle rules the world."

For those of you who are full-time mothers and concerned about your position in life, take the words of Lucille Ball to heart: "If you raise successful children, it is your greatest source of happiness. If your children are unsuccessful, no success you have will ever make you happy."

P.S. Many women have been made to feel "less than" for their choice to stay home and be full-time mothers. In a marriage and other intimate relationships, it would help us so much if men could help boost our self-esteem and self-confidence in this role. Some of you men may be experiencing this "stay-at-home" role as well. Deborah and I have friends who are living in reversed roles within their marriage, with the wife being the sole breadwinner and the husband staying home to manage the household and care for the children. Let's remember to acknowledge the unique contribution each of us is making in our lives, and dare to believe in our dreams no matter what role we are currently in.

● ● ●

And your family can't take all the blame for how we working women feel about ourselves. In an article in *USA Today,* demographer Cheryl Russell pointed out that the media also put pressure on women. Fears about the breakup of the family lead to stories about how fashionable it has become to be a stay-at-home mother. Gushing reporters tell us how many women have given up their careers to be with their children.

These stories, coupled with the hair-raising statistics about young children committing horrendous crimes, teenagers out of control and family values disappearing, all work to add to the incredible guilt laid on women.

But don't get us wrong. We agree with Dr. Laura Scheslinger that little kids and big kids need to be nurtured and raised by two parents, if possible, who spend as much time as humanly possible being parents. Children need to be raised as children. Not as pets, who are exercised and given a treat by the owners who feel guilty leaving them home alone so much.

However, Cheryl Russell pointed out that according to a *Redbook* survey, 57 percent of mothers who have children under 18 do not want their marriage to be like that of their parents. Most feel they're parenting as well as their parents did, or even better. Nine out of ten women think their family today is happier than the one they grew up in, even though today almost two-thirds of working women are mothers.

Life Is a Self-Fulfilling Prophecy

As with every characteristic of successful people, there are also two sides to self-expectancy—positive and negative. There are those who use negative expectation to invite the unwanted into their lives.

The woman who says, "My child always gets sick the day before we go on vacation," can count on the fact she will be serving up chicken soup and popsicles when she planned to be on the beach.

We've all known someone who worried because one of their parents had a heart attack and died at an early age— and sure enough, they also die at about the same age. That's negative expectation.

• • •

Denis: But what does all this have to do with positive self-expectation and the psychology of winning? Simply this: Mental obsessions do have physical manifestations. Just as you become what you think about, you become that which you fear. You get out of life just about what you expect to get, and you become what you expect to be. This power of the self-fulfilling prophecy is one of the most amazing phenomena of human nature.

Positive people, who have a solid sense of their own worth, believe in themselves totally. Against incredible odds, they believe they can accomplish the seemingly impossible—and heaven help anyone who tries to stand in their way!

When you expect the best, you fashion the future to make the expectation come true. How you put together that future is up to you, but we have suggested keeping a journal because it has worked for so many people.

• • •

Tammy Lilly was the captain of the Olympic women's volleyball team that won the bronze medal in Barcelona in 1992. Like many of her fellow athletes, she has designed her current training and her future plans in her daily journal. She advises, "If you look at your journal every day, it helps you remember what you need to do, and keeps you on track."

Here's something we'd like you to think about. You may want to write your thoughts about it in your journal. What do you expect for yourself?

Notice that we didn't ask, "What do you want for yourself?" This has nothing to do with the old daydream of winning the lottery and having every material thing you could ever wish for. No, in this case you need to think about what you expect for yourself—and you should expect the best.

If you're truly successful, you believe that you're responsible for your own self-fulfilling prophecies. You keep your momentum high. You expect to advance in your job and receive more money in your paycheck. You expect to be healthy and live a long time. You expect to live in a warm and loving family, enjoying financial security. You expect your friends to like you as much as you like them.

It's too bad that so many of us have trouble believing in the kind of future we really want. Merle Shain said, "The conflict between what one is—and who one is expected to be—touches all of us. And sometimes, rather than reach for what one could be, we choose the comfort of the failed role, preferring to be a victim of circumstance, the person who didn't have a chance."

More than men, women work their lives around the needs of others. Our husbands, children and aging parents take precedence over our own desires. Too often women say, "I'll take up tennis when my husband retires," or "Maybe I can go back to college after my children are grown," or "I plan to travel when my parents don't need me so much."

Unfortunately, when we say "I do" to another person, we often say "I won't" to ourselves. We become afraid of success because it might take us away from home or keep us working late at night or upset the balance with our partner. Success means change, and change means adjustments that may be hard to make.

• • •

Deborah: A huge challenge in my life has been to overcome the expectations of others and dare to believe in myself. As the firstborn of an achievement-oriented, ex-Navy pilot father and a professional singer, stage-oriented mother, I found myself pulled in two different directions. From the time I was a young child, the expectations placed upon me were very high. I was the dutiful daughter who strove to please her parents by getting straight As every year for my father and taking ballet, modern dance, tap, swimming, tennis, and music lessons for my mother. As I grew older I felt an underlying tension, perhaps my own projection of not living up to the expectations of being a Stanford or Harvard graduate for my father and an academy award-winning actress or Grammy winner for my mother.

I realized the disappointment I felt about not living up to my parents' expectations was really directed at myself—for not living up to my own. I hadn't given myself the chance to discover what my own expectations for my life were. It was time to dare to believe—in myself. I wrote entries in my journal about how I had come to lead a life that was not my own. It became obvious to me that if I didn't identify what my true expectations were for my life, I would never meet them. It was time to write my own script, not live someone else's, and earn my own As in the areas of life that appealed to me.

P.S. In the area of expectations, especially those imposed on you by others, I offer the utmost empathy to all of you men. I think you have been exposed to a plethora of expectations, such as carrying on the family name, the family business, becoming president, etc.—things that women were not typically expected to do. In your own way you must also rise up to the challenge of breaking free of parental and societal expectations and dare to believe in yourself!

● ● ●

Among the ancient scriptures is this thought: "Your work is to discover your work, and then with all your heart to give yourself to it." That work may not be a career in the traditional sense. It may be the work of mothering your children, volunteering to your community, or writing books that touch the lives of others. It may involve serving meals to the elderly, working in the literacy program, or walking through your neighborhood every day picking up trash. However you help another, you help yourself times ten.

Tap Your Hidden Resources

Barbara Gordon is a television producer. She feels that "Every person has his or her own safe place—running, painting, swimming, fishing, weaving, gardening. The activity is less important than the act of drawing on your own resources."

The nature of the work isn't important. What matters is that you find your purpose on this earth and fulfill it. In the ebb and flow of the earth's rhythm, your particular purpose has its own special note to play, and that note is important to the rest of the music. Often, major changes have been brought about by seemingly insignificant activities. And if, like many of us, you feel your purpose isn't that important to the scheme of things, remember what the English entrepreneur Anita Koddick wrote: "If you think you're too small to have an impact, try going to bed with a mosquito."

We've all heard about Helen Keller. She'd been deaf and blind since infancy, yet she graduated from college magna cum laude and devoted her life to the service of others. Thanks to her indomitable spirit—and the patient coaching of her teacher, Anne Sullivan—she maintained a positive, upbeat attitude toward life and became a role model to millions. She used to say, "No pessimist ever discovered the secrets of the stars, or sailed to an uncharted land, or opened a new heaven to the human spirit."

While Helen Keller's story is familiar, what we don't know is how much her success was influenced by a woman named Laura Bridgman. Like Helen, Laura became totally blind and deaf because of a childhood disease. Laura had even more to overcome because she was also rendered mute and lost most of her sense of taste and touch. Until she was seven, she drifted along without help. Then Dr. Samuel Howe, the director of the Perkins Institute for the Blind in Watertown, Massachusetts, heard about her case and took her under his care. Within a short time, Laura was writing letters. Later she began writing poetry, and then her autobiography. Finally she joined the faculty at the Perkins Institute as a teacher.

So how did she influence Helen Keller? Laura's case inspired Anne Sullivan. When she realized how far Laura Bridgman had progressed, Anne knew that the young Helen Keller, who was not as physically restricted, could go even further. Never forget, even though we may not know it, each of us has a profound influence on other people.

How we live our lives influences how others may expect to live theirs to match the model we project. Our achievements give them permission to optimistically expect to do better than we ever dreamed.

• • •

Denis: There's more to positive self-expectancy than what shows on the surface. Medical researchers have discovered that the body produces endorphins, which are natural, morphine-like substances that operate on certain receptor sites in the brain and spinal cord.

Endorphins are secreted in the brain, which uses them to reduce the impact of unwelcome experiences and screen out unpleasant stimuli. The presence of endorphins in the body actually produces a feeling of well-being.

In one study, actors were wired to electrodes and connected to blood catheters before they were asked to perform various scenes. When they portrayed characters who were angry or depressed, their endorphin levels dropped. But when a scene called for emoting joy, confidence and love, their endorphin level shot up dramatically.

The good news is, endorphins work both ways. It's called "a win-win situation." They're nature's own mood-altering drug. Science has shown that positive thoughts produce endorphins. Endorphins, in turn, encourage feelings of optimism and well-being. You sing because you're happy, and you're happier because you sing. When you're negative, your endorphin level goes down. When you're upbeat and positive, your endorphin level goes up. So all you have to do is change your attitude.

That's why it's critically important to remember that the key to winning self-expectation is for each of us to understand that in the long run we receive just about what we expect, and we build our lives to reach what we expect we can have. When optimistic expectation has become a way of life, you'll be rewarded accordingly.

● ● ●

Positive Self-Expectancy Action Steps

Let's go through some techniques for generating a greater attitude of positive self-expectancy so you can plan the optimum outcome for your life.

1. Replace the word "problem" in your vocabulary with the word "challenge," and look at each challenge as an opportunity. Always search for what's good in every situation.

2. Make a determined effort to stay relaxed and friendly, no matter how much pressure and tension you're under. At first you may have to fake it. But the truth is that both calmness and courage are learned habits, and there's no better way to learn a good habit than by actually jumping in and doing it.

3. When you're dealing with other people, try praising instead of complaining. In place of cynicism, try optimism. Instead of being unhelpfully critical, try being constructively helpful. These are also learned habits, and it's never too late to start developing them. Each of us is dependent on others for at least part of our own self-expectancy.

If all we ever hear is negative feedback, discouraging outlooks and critical comments, we'll be tempted to withdraw into the cocoon of complacency and let the world pass us by without so much as a wave in our direction.

4. Be excited and enthusiastic about your own dream. This excitement is like a forest fire—you can smell it, taste it, and see it a mile away. Everybody loves a successful person. They want to be near a winner. They want to shake her hand and have pictures taken standing by her side. But nobody crowds around the loser.

So don't run around with the doomsayers who look up and shout that the sky is always falling. Optimism and realism are the problem-solving twins. At the same time, pessimism and cynicism are the two worst companions you can choose.

Colette Dowling says, "The woman who has sprung free has emotional mobility. She is able to move toward the things that are satisfying to her and away from those that are not. She is free, also, to succeed."

In the next chapter, we'll talk about positive self-image, which provides the vision and clarity that enables us to go from dreams to reality.

POPULAR MYTHS	TRUTH OF THE MATTER
• "You're too old to change."	• "You can replace bad habits with good ones, regardless of your age."
• "You have to earn your value because you aren't worth much."	• "You are born with infinite value."
• "Go for the jugular; winning is beating."	• "If you go for the jugular, you cut what counts— your own throat."
• "Why dream? You're stuck with what you have."	• "You are not your genes and environment."
• "Nice girls finish last."	• "Nice girls usually finish best."
• "Do it to others, before they do it to you."	• "Do it for others, and they will commit to you and be there for you."
• "Don't stick your neck out."	• "Failure is the fertilizer of success."
• "You either have it or you don't."	• "Your attitude is the key to your door of success."
• "Luck is in the stars."	• "Luck is laboring under correct knowledge."
• "Whatever will be will be."	• "If it is to be, it's up to me."
• "Thank God it's Friday."	• "Thank God it's Today."

Chapter 7

●

Dream Your Reality

The next characteristic of a total achiever is self-imagination. Self-imagination is different from self-acceptance. Self-acceptance is knowing your strengths and
weaknesses and being comfortable with both. Self-confidence is liking and trusting yourself. Self-motivation is having a passionate desire for excellence inside that moves you
to action. Self-espectancy is optimism. And self-imagination is seeing specifically who you want to be in the future.

● ● ●

Denis: All winners in life develop and actively think
about a positive self-image. The scenes you portray in your
imagination are often more than mere fantasies. Often they
are previews of coming attractions in your life, as surely as if
you were looking into a crystal ball and forecasting your
future. Just as the words of positive self-talk have a profound
impact on your self-confidence and self-motivation, so does
what you visualize in your mind's eye have a profound impact
on your self-image and the achievement of your goals. You
see, individuals don't behave in accordance with reality but
in accordance with their own learned "virtual" reality.

Virtual because some of it is handed down as hearsay and
second-hand experience from the past, and *virtual* because
some of it is fantasy or premonition about something that has

135

not actually occurred yet, or may never occur in the future. When you change your self-image, you change your outlook and your behavior, and thus alter your destiny.

• • •

Imagination Rules the World

Our great-grandmother used to say we shouldn't worry about scores on IQ tests. We should view our IQs as Imagination Quotients rather than a measure of intelligence.

True vision is inner vision, an ability to convert past experience into positive input and to visualize a desired future. People who can do this become leaders, many also attaining great wealth. Storing every transaction as a learning opportunity, keeping their vision unclouded by negativism from past setbacks, they can see their missions clearly and describe them vividly. Visionaries, who can see clearly what the future can look like, attract resources, believers, and followers.

• • •

Dayna: As a child I learned about the power of the imagination and how to turn dreams into reality. At age eleven, I wanted a dog more than anything else in the world. I already had a menagerie of hamsters, parakeets, and guinea pigs, but I longed for an animal that would be a real companion and friend. I began saving all my allowance money and buying all the things necessary for the care and feeding of my future dog.

My parents first caught on to my plans when my father stubbed his toe on what he thought was a large metal Frisbee lying on the kitchen floor. "Who put this land mine in front of the refrigerator?" he howled at us kids while we were eating our cereal. I proudly answered, "I did, Dad. That's my dog's dish."

"How can that be your dog's dish, when we don't have a dog?" he retorted.

"He's my imaginary dog, Dad. But he's becoming so real that I had to buy his dish this week, so we can feed him when he gets here!" I blurted out excitedly.

"That dish is big enough for a horse, and besides, we're not getting a dog right now, period," he scolded.

Later that day, I began walking around the yard talking to a long chain I was dragging behind my back.

"What are you doing, talking to yourself with that piece of chain in your hand?" Dad inquired.

"It's my dog leash, and I'm practicing taking him for a walk," I corrected. He told me to practice in my room because the neighbors might be watching, and they thought we were a bit strange already.

My dad knew he had been a little bit gruff on the dog issue, and he tried to smooth things out by acting interested in my goal. "If you did get a dog, at some future date, what kind of dog would you get, honey," he inquired softly, "a yorkie or a poodle?"

"Well, actually, Dad, my dog is an Alaskan Malamute," I explained. He reminded me that we lived in Southern California, and that the poor dog would pant and shed its fur all summer long. "And besides," he added, "he probably would smell!"

I had a one-track mind. "You're right, Dad," I replied, "Alaskan Malamutes have great noses. He'll always find his way back home, and he'll be a great watchdog, you'll see."

I then pulled out a little pocket book titled *The Care and Feeding of Alaskan Malamutes* and flipped through the pages. "You'll learn to love Kheemo, Dad," I said confidently. "I got his name from the *Lone Ranger* TV show. It's an abbreviation for the name Kheemosabe (Kheemo-sah-beh), which is an Indian expression meaning 'good friend.'"

The next day was Father's Day. I knew it was going to be a special day, all right.

Dad came down the stairs in his pajamas, robe, and slippers, with the *TV Guide* in one hand and the morning paper in the other. "Today, I am going to concentrate on doing absolutely nothing. I'm going to stay in my bathrobe, relax, and watch baseball and movies all day," he announced.

Dad noticed that all of us kids were dressed as if we were going on an outing. He opened his Father's Day card, and taped at the bottom, after all the endearing poetry, was a classified ad from the morning paper:

"Last of the litter. One adorable AKC male Alaskan Malamute puppy. Purebred, papers, shots. Only $500. Drive by today. This one won't last. Ideal children's pet."

"Don't you want to take your children for a drive on Father's Day?" we chimed in together.

"As a matter of fact, that's exactly what I don't want to do," he retorted, sticking his nose in the *TV Guide* to see what time the game came on. Our response was well-rehearsed and coached by our mother, and it sounded like something out of Harry Chapin's classic song, "The Cat's in the Cradle."

"That's OK, Dad, don't be blue, 'cause we're gonna grow up just like you," we chanted. "Someday when you're old and gray, you'll want us to visit you on Father's Day," we continued. "You'll say, 'Come over kids and visit me,' but we'll say, 'Sorry, Dad, we're watching TV.' Oh, that's OK, Dad, don't be blue, 'cause we're gonna grow up just like you."

The dog cost $500. The fence cost $500. He ate the webbing off the patio furniture. He destroyed the flower garden. He chewed up Dad's house slippers and his best jogging shoes. But Kheemo finally grew up to be a fine family pet and watchdog. I now believe in my dreams. But I realize how important it is to have someone to help you reach your goals.

• • •

What we imagine is what we become. Although the popular adage is "never cross a bridge until you come to it," the most successful people in our world have crossed those bridges in their imaginations long before they ever saw them.

As Mary Richards says, "The imagination equips us to perceive reality when it is not fully materialized."

And what a wonderful reality that can be! At 14, Sandra Day O'Connor pondered a career in lawmaking while visiting state capitals during summer vacation. She became the first woman justice of the U.S. Supreme Court. A divorced grandmother from the inner city of Milwaukee saw herself leading her country, and Golda Meir became the first woman prime minister of Israel. Maggie Thatcher dreamed of leading England at the age of 21 in her father's one-room flat over their grocery store. An awkward, nondescript girl in New York was totally obsessed with becoming a professional entertainer. She grew into Barbra Streisand.

As the 20th of 21 children, she had a withered leg and couldn't walk without leg braces until she was 12. She became the first triple-gold-medalist in women's Olympic track history: the fastest woman in the world at the Rome Olympics, Wilma Rudolph.

If you've any doubts about the power of self-image, talk to someone who has lost a part of his or her body. Amputee patients commonly experience pain, itching, or tingling in the empty spaces where the hands, legs, arms, or feet had been. During the night, it's not uncommon for double amputees to try to get out of bed and walk, realizing only after they have fallen that they their legs are no longer there.

All that remains is the pain and sensation where the limbs had been. This is known as the "ghost limb." It's one of the great mysteries of the human mind and nervous system. How do we experience sensations, not of what's happening in reality, but of what we're conditioned to feel before the reality changed?

The medical explanation for this phenomenon is that nerve fibers at the point of amputation grow new connections, and these are what activate the brain. Since adult neurons don't regenerate, a team of scientists at Vanderbilt University, headed up by Dr. Sherre Florence, is studying the "phantom" sensations to see if somehow they can stimulate this rewiring effect when they want it—for instance, in the case of stroke victims.

We Set Our Own Limits

Without realizing it, we've developed a self-image concerning every talent we have, every sensitivity we show, and every action we perform. Listen to how people talk about themselves: "I'm such a lousy cook, I can't even use the microwave oven." "I have a great sense of humor." "I have a terrible memory." "I make smart business decisions." "I'm a warm and sensitive person." "I'll never get through that math class." "When it comes to computers, I'm roadkill on the information superhighway." "I can see it for *you*, but not for *me*."

• • •

Denis: Whether we're aware of it or not, each of us is controlled by these mental pictures we form. We can't outgrow the limits we place on ourselves. All we can do is set new limits within which we must live. Let's repeat that, because we want to be very sure you grasp it, and you'll probably want to write it in your journal.

140

—————————•—————————

We can never outgrow the limits we place on ourselves. We can only set new limits within which we must live.

Our self-image, which dwells at the subconscious level of thinking, determines the kind and scope of person we are in every walk of life. Although the term "subconscious mind" has been used, often inaccurately by nonprofessional people, it's more correct to think of it not as a mind, but rather as a level of awareness with very special characteristics and abilities.

Let's imagine two levels of thinking, using the analogy of a money bank, with a cardholder and an ATM machine. The cardholder is the conscious level of thinking. It's responsible for collecting information from all around us, storing it in our memory bank, and making rational decisions.

And the ATM machine is the subconscious level of thinking, responsible for autonomic body control, such as breathing and heartbeat, and the storage of information and creative goal-seeking in long-term memory.

Like the subconscious level of thinking in your brain, the ATM machine at your bank is programmed to perform a number of specific tasks. When the cardholder activates it by punching in the code, the machine does exactly what it's told to do.

The human brain operates in much the same way but is far more elegant and complex than any system we could ever invent. Compared to the human brain-mind system, the biggest Cray super-computer is like a speck of dust.

Let's look at the relationship of the conscious, cardholder level and the subconscious, ATM-level of thinking. The cardholder can't make a decision—she can't withdraw money, transfer funds, deposit or get account information—until she clears it with the ATM machine. The ATM checks its memory bank and then replays available data back to the cardholder for action. If you notice, this is one case where the machine controls the human. Unless the ATM gives you permission, you can't make a transaction.

In the same way, our subconscious mind controls our conscious level of thinking. Action frequently takes place without consultation with the cardholder, but no action ever takes place without reference to the ATM.

The information that's fed into your ATM's memory bank stays there, waiting for you to retrieve it. You can never willfully erase the information. You are able to override it or modify it over a period of time, but like a notation on your credit history, you're virtually stuck with the information for life.

The Automatic Teller: Your Self-Image

There's an automatic teller inside you and me,
A subconscious bank statement of what we hear and see;
It makes positive deposits of praise and love and cheer,
And negative withdrawals of abuse and hate and fear.
It doesn't care what's right or wrong, or what is false or true,
It's the servant of all great leaders, and all the failures too;
It's this automatic teller that builds your life success,
It's the day-to-day deposits that lead to happiness.
Be careful of the inputs and images you store,
Be wise with your role models and the heroes you adore;
It's this automatic teller, the self-image that we hold,
That takes the ore of compound thoughts and forges it to gold.
Before you go to sleep tonight, let her know how much you care,
Be sure she feels the value of the love you have to share.
For there's nothing more important to the future that she'll live,
Than the automatic teller and the deposits that you give!

Just as we sometimes feel as if our lives are run by the ATM machine, we're slaves to our subconscious, which houses our all-important self-image. If you try to use willpower to make a change in yourself at the conscious level, usually the change will be only temporary. This is why so many people have trouble losing weight. They want to diet, and they impose their will power on their subconscious. But if the window in the ATM shows you a balance that says "fat," your body will struggle to maintain that self-image, and you'll be fighting a losing battle.

Just as the only way to avoid a negative balance in your savings account is to make consistent deposits, the only way to overcome any bad habit is to reprogram your subconscious with new healthy images.

● ● ●

Our Own Virtual Reality

Current research in the neuro-sciences using CAT-scans, PET-scans, and MRI's (Magnetic Resonance Imaging) confirms that vividly repeated, imagined experience as well as actual experience is stored in long-term memory as present-tense, real-time activity. When it is replayed, it is relived as if were actually happening in the here and now, with all the sensory feelings of touch, smell, taste, sounds, and pictures.

Since the self-image stored in long-term memory doesn't have any judging function, it tries to meet the objectives and goals we set before it without concerning itself about their merit. It doesn't matter whether these goals are negative or positive, wrong or right, factual or fantasy, non-dangerous or dangerous, losing or winning. Its sole function is to follow instructions based on previous inputs—like a computer reading its hard drive or CD-ROM and responding automatically.

The good news is that the human brain can beat the mechanical memory. This was proven again recently when the most technologically advanced IBM computer, known

143

as Deep Blue, was programmed with the most sophisticated chess playing ability and pitted against Gary Kasparov, the Russian chess grand master and world champion. At first, the computer won. But within a few games, Kasparov had figured out the machine's strategy and changed his own game to be unpredictable.

The computer was hopelessly checkmated after that. Since your subconscious self-image is totally predictable in that it always follows previous instructions, you can override it by entering new information and layering it on top of the old program. You can't erase what's there, but you can replace it over time.

Behavioral scientists agree that your subconscious self-image can't distinguish between actual and virtual experience. The subconscious stores emotional fantasies as your own reality. Many of your everyday decisions are based upon information about yourself that has been stored as truth but is nothing more than a figment of your own imagination, shaded by your environmental conditioning.

Unfortunately, in the case of "false memory syndrome," some crimes are "remembered" even though they never occurred, and lives are ruined because of the power of suggestion of well-meaning authorities and counselors. It's not unusual to hear someone recant an accusation of childhood abuse, usually too late to restore the good name of the person accused. By the same token, many valid cases are swept under the rug because they're assumed only to be hysterically imagined reality, when they actually occurred and were imbedded in repressed memory because of the trauma at the time the event took place.

Reset Your Dream Machine

As children, we had fantasies about what we wanted to be when we grew up—entertainer, scientist, world leader, parent, astronaut, entrepreneur. We tried on numerous roles during our play-filled days of childhood and our dream-filled days of adolescence. Each role, job, or successful accomplishment seemed equally possible to us and equally real in our imaginations.

As we grew older, we began to narrow the possibilities. Some careers seemed beyond our reach. We were advised—or ill-advised as the case might be—by parents, teachers, others adults, or even our friends that we couldn't be, shouldn't be or wouldn't be extremely successful.

Too often, our possibilities were narrowed by ourselves or by our choice to believe the limiting opinions of others, to the point of our living with a tightly compressed self-image. The vast fertile fields of our lives began to shrink from the image of a towering redwood tree in our mind's eye until we saw our future plot of success as being "flower-pot" in size. Suddenly, most of the world seemed impossible or inaccessible to us—in our imaginations.

The critical point to recognize, of course, is that both the unlimited potential of childhood and the tight constraints of adulthood originate and reside primarily in the imagination. It's time to reset the dream machine and adjust the dials in favor of towering growth and abundance.

● ● ●

Denis: "Dream" is a very important word to remember. We've all heard the line from the song, "A dream is a wish your heart makes." Our longtime friend and motivational speaker, Zig Ziglar, says, "A goal is a dream with a deadline."

From the time he was a young boy, Jim Carrey knew what he wanted to do with his life. At age 10, the comic actor of such hits as "The Mask," and "The Truman Show," was making funny faces in the mirror at his home in Canada. Comedy was his inevitable path. Throughout his childhood, there were many bumpy roads.

They lost their house and were forced to live in a camper and later in a tent. When Jim turned 19 and wanted to pursue show business full-time, what did he have to lose? And besides, his father encouraged him to go after his dream.

Three years later, Jim Carrey was making money, but unhappy, doing impressions in Las Vegas as a warmup act. He finally convinced the club owner to let him try his comedy act, and he was an instant hit. Five years before he became a movie star, Carrey wrote himself a check for $10 million and postdated it, Thanksgiving 1995. Incredibly, his personal fortune grew to that amount during that time.

"I wrote the check as an affirmation of everything I've learned," he said. "It wasn't about money. I knew if I was making that much, I'd be working with the best people using the best material. That's always been my dream. Better to risk starving than surrender. If you give up on your dream, what's left?"

● ● ●

Set aside a section of your journal where you can let your imagination go without restraint, and write down your wildest dreams. They may seem improbable at this moment in your life, but when you write them down, you give them credence and life.

The poet Maya Angelou wrote, "If one is lucky, a solitary fantasy can totally transform one million realities." And the early feminist and social reformer Emma Goldman said, "When we cannot dream any longer, we die."

Dream Your Reality

———•———

Many women tell us that they are afraid to dream because they don't want to be disappointed when their dreams don't come true. There's so much of the little child in that belief. The stories of Cinderella, Sleeping Beauty, and Snow White are just that—stories.

In real life, we have to go out and grab our dreams by the throat and wrestle them into our lives. Just wishing doesn't work if you want to be an achiever. However, the greater the dream—the more concrete the goal, the more positive your self-esteem—then the more certain you are to win.

Sarah Ban Breathnach in her inspiring book, *Simple Abundance*, writes: "Dreams are gifts of Spirit meant to alter us. Trust that the same Power that gifted you with your dream knows how to help you make it come true."

• • •

Deborah: On my 39th birthday I decided to reset my dream machine. After all, with only one year left before becoming, according to society's standards, an "older woman," I thought I'd better hurry up and give life all I had left of my youth. At the top of a page in my journal I wrote the words "My Wildest Dream" and unleashed my imagination.

Within a few minutes my mind soared to a huge arena with thousands of people applauding where I was performing and singing on a large stage. It was dark all around me except for the colors of the stage lights and a beam of light shining from above. I could make out faces in the crowd, and our eyes met. Ah yes, my wildest dream . . . Returning to the reality of my open journal, I wrote down two more words: "Rock" and "Star." I laughed out loud and rolled my eyes as two additional words overrode the previous ones: "Yeah" and "Right."

But something was awakened in me. This dream had made its way from the cellars of my subconsicous to the light of my conscious mind and was made visible on the journal page. I signed up for vocal lessons and set aside time each day to practice vocal exercises and guitar chords. I had sung in public only a few times before: church choir, middle school choir and a couple of family weddings. I was terrified of performing, but I visualized myself poised and calm on an imaginary stage. I saved some money and bought an acoustic performance amplifier, which allowed me to mike my voice and amplify the guitar. I felt like a real performer and pictured myself playing in public. During this time I was living in a studio apartment, too small for adequate musical expression. I rented a small studio space for $100 per month. The manager told me Jewel had practiced there before she became famous. In front of a large mirror in the studio room, I practiced performing and dreamed of one day singing in front of a large audience just like her.

I battled constantly with my inner critic and the judgmental voices of "you're too old," "this is crazy," "you can't start a music career this late in life," "you're not any good," "you have no experience," and so on. But I was fueled by my dream. Every night before going to sleep I wrote about my progress toward my dream. Ten months later, on a whim, I answered an ad in the local newspaper: "Wanted, back-up female vocalist with some guitar experience for adult rock/alternative band working on CD and live performance projects." Two weeks later, as a full-fledged member of "Diamond in the Rough," I was playing a live gig at a local coffeehouse. My dream reached its zenith another ten months later on the stage of an outdoor amphitheater to a soldout summer crowd, opening for "Three Dog Night," one of my favorite bands back in middle school when I was singing in the choir. It was dark all around me, except for the colors of the stage lights and a beam of white light that shone from above, a full moon. I could make out the faces in the crowd, and our eyes met. They were part of my dream, which was now a reality. We later recorded a CD, performed to thousands of people at Sea World, and played on the strip in Las Vegas. Never underestimate the power of your dreams—no matter how wild or seemingly impossible.

• • •

"The Power of Dreaming" Journal Exercise

Here are some exercises to help you tap into the power of dreaming. First, find pictures that represent your dreams and goals, and paste them in your journal. These can be pictures of the body you want to have, the trip you want to take, the house you want to live in, the new outfit you want to buy. Keep looking at the pictures and visualizing yourself in them. This will help you internalize your dreams, making them real and attainable.

Second, make it an important project to seek out and talk this week to someone who's currently doing what you want to do most. This applies whether you're talking about selling, managing, skiing, traveling, speaking, redecorating, or even being a good spouse or parent.

The expert you're looking for may be next door, across town or in another part of the country. Surf the net. Attend lectures and talk to the speaker afterward. Participate in courses at the adult learning centers that are found in most major cities. Find courses to take from the extension program at your local university. Do whatever you need to find an expert and get the facts.

Make a project of learning everything you can about other winners in your area of interest. As Eleanor Roosevelt said, "The future belongs to those who believe in the beauty of their dreams." Since your behavior or achievement level is usually consistent with your self-image, it will play a large part in how well you adapt to the new world.

Your self-image operates much the way a thermostat controls the temperature in your house. You set the thermostat at 72 degrees, which is comfortable for you. When the temperature in the room dips below the setting, the thermostat automatically triggers the furnace to come on until 72 degrees is reached again. If the temperature gets too high, the furnace shuts off until the temperature again reaches your comfort zone of 72 degrees.

It works the same way with your self-image and achievement. If you perform below your self-image level, you'll get uncomfortable and make an adjustment to do better next time. If you perform too well or too high above your self-image setting, tension will automatically bring your performance back down to where your imagination tells you it belongs. This explains why some of us have temporary success and then sabotage ourselves because we start choking under pressure.

In your journal, make some notes about your response to these questions. Do you view your self-image as your life handicap, or is it your achievement mechanism? Are you a lifetime slave to your ATM machine? Or do you control the balance by making positive deposits consistently?

The Champion Within

The achievers in life control the balance and change it only when they want to. With time and effort, they elevate their self-image and enlarge their universe.

Achievers hold onto the self-image of the person they'd most like to become. They get a vivid, clear, emotional, sensory picture of themselves, as if they'd already achieved their new role in life They know their subconscious can't tell the difference between "the real me and the one I see."

Achievers see themselves sitting in the boardroom. They hear the audience applause. They ride the Queen's float in the Rose Bowl Parade. They can feel the solid gold weight of the medal around their neck while the National Anthem plays. They touch the diploma in their hand at graduation, in advance.

They can picture the bank balance that is the financial reward of success. They relish the self-esteem resulting from their personal achievement. Because achievers feel like they're successful, they look at the world through the eyes of a champion.

What do you see for you today? Who will you be tomorrow?

• • •

Denis: We'd like to give you a couple of personal exercises to help you build a more positive self-image.

First, set aside a time each day, while you take a shower or dress or drive to work or exercise, to imagine yourself achieving and enjoying your most important, creative personal desires. Pretend you're previewing television short subjects. Picture one sequence accomplishing a professional triumph, maybe a promotion, a bonus or an award ceremony.

Picture another scene involving family success, maybe a special outing, a reunion or a trip abroad. And still another in which you're relishing a personal, private victory, possibly a fitness goal, a sports championship, or learning a new skill.

Get the actual sensation and clear image of each event and how good it feels to experience each one. Learn the art of transformation into your new role, which we call the "Meryl Streep Role Reversal."

For many years, this brilliant actress has assumed roles of unfulfilled women, enduring great hardships. We want you to use her technique, only in reverse.

For nearly an hour before filming her scene in the movie *Ironweed* many years ago, in which she plays a ragged outcast during the Depression who dies in a cheap hotel room, Meryl hugged a giant bag of ice cubes to simulate the feeling of lifelessness. In the scene, her hobo lover, played by Jack Nicholson, cried and sobbed, shaking her body. After the cameras had stopped, the film crew panicked because Meryl continued to lay there cold and still.

She can actually vanish into another person, looking, speaking, thinking, moving and feeling like the characters she plays. Director Mike Nichols says, "She changes who she is and casts a spell over other members of the cast. As she becomes the person she is portraying, the other actors begin to react to her as if she were that person. She changes the chemistry of all the relationships because she is endowed with the magnificent powers of self-imagination and transformation."

Like Meryl Streep, you—in real life—can look, think, move, feel and be the roles you want to assume and the goals you want to achieve."

You can literally become the person you're portraying. Only in your case, it won't be acting in a difficult part. It will be a preview of coming positive attractions. And the person you see in the mirror of your mind will be a woman who is winning her greatest personal triumphs.

The second suggestion is to read a biography every two months, six a year, of someone who has reached the top in your profession or in your major passion, or someone you have admired for his or her courage. If you don't have time to read, pick up the audio cassette of the book and listen in the car or while you do chores or exercise. And as you read or listen, imagine yourself as that person. Step into the starring role.

Look through the book review sections in newspapers and magazines, and keep a list in your journal of the books you want to read. Then put a big star next to those you've finished. Read fiction as well as nonfiction books. While nonfiction biographies give you the courage and knowledge to believe in your own ability to succeed, reading fiction stimulates your imagination. Watching television does not. Television provides all the graphics and imagery, without your involvement. Reading fiction novels puts you in the story, which is why when the movie is made you don't recognize the characters. They're not the ones you have created in your mind.

As we move from childhood into adulthood, most of us "lock up" our imaginative powers because we can't imagine drawing pictures outside the lines. Many teenagers and young adults have given up on seeking the American Dream because they can't place themselves in a success scenario. They are stuck in the sitcoms and tabloids. They've accepted the image of mediocrity, frustration, problems with no solutions, and diminishing opportunities. This is the "video" they have planted in their minds.

The key to excellence is a commitment to lifelong learning, which may once have been a luxury. You can't compete today if your understanding of change is erroneous, incomplete, misinformed, or outdated.

• • •

Stretch Your Limits

No matter what your profession or position, you must "Incorporate Yourself Mentally." Begin to think of yourself as "Me, Incorporated," a management services company with one employee—you. In an era of downsizing, out-sourcing, reengineering and reorganization, you must increase your knowledge base, vocabulary, and communication skills to adapt rapidly to new global market demands.

If you want to do something that may take some training and you're worried about your age, consider this: In a few years, you will be a few years older, with or without the experience behind you. What's really stopping you from doing what's in your heart?

Consider Sister Mary Martin Weaver, a Catholic nun, who took up athletics many years ago after age 55. At last count, she had won more than 50 gold, silver, and bronze medals in the Rocky Mountain Senior Games and the U. S. National Senior Olympics. Her specialties include speed and figure skating, ice hockey, snowshoe racing, the 5,000-meter race-walk, shotput, and basketball freethrows. Move over Michael Jordan—Sister Mary may get the big endorsement contract!

"People have gotten flabby", she says, "and I don't mean just physically. Anything that's challenging, people just don't want to do. But there are no rewards in anything unless you try. Age should never be a barrier to full participation in life. What's most important is to enjoy life to its fullest, to do things for and with others, and never, ever be afraid to stretch your limits. Choose to win!"

Thank you, Sister Mary. You are a tough act to follow.

You also may have heard of Sheryl Leach, a former teacher, who was taking care of her two-year-old son back in 1987 when she realized she couldn't find any nurturing videos to entertain him. So she sat down and wrote the script for one herself, first about a teddy bear, and then, inspired by a traveling dinosaur exhibit that had come to town, about a Tyrannosaurus Rex.

She recruited another former teacher, as well as a video producer and a bunch of neighborhood kids, and created a video from her scripts. Today, "Barney," the purple dinosaur, is a billion-dollar industry.

The point isn't that Sheryl is a mega-millionaire. The point is—what if she had been afraid to pursue her dream? She would have been a redwood tree stuck in a flowerpot, too old or too timid or too root- bound to get out and grow! Growing up should mean just that, growing up as tall as we can in our vision and reach. Dream the biggest dream you can. Imagination becomes realization.

In the next chapter, we'll discuss the characteristic of self-direction: turning dreams into goals, plans, and priorities.

Five Action Steps to a Better Self-Image

1. Set your own internal standards instead of comparing yourself to others.

2. Accept yourself as you are right now, but keep upgrading your standards, lifestyle, behavior, professional training, and relationships by associating with winners.

3. Project your best self. Dressing well and looking your best do not have to be trendy fashions and designer labels. Being appropriate for the occasion and being neat and clean are more important. Personal grooming and apprearance provide an instantaneous projection on the surface of how you feel inside about yourself.

4. Visualize your future consistent with your principles and values. If there's a conflict, you'll be less likely to get your mind and body working in concert. Ask yourself if what you are picturing is really in your own best interest and in the best interest of those who will be affected.

5. Most important, when you visualize yourself, see yourself in the present, as if you are already accomplishing your goal. Make certain your visual image is as you would see it through your own eyes, not watching through the eyes of a spectator. If you're a skier, your imagery would appear in your mind as if an invisible TV camera were mounted on your shoulder looking exactly where your eyes are focused during a ski run, and you would be feeling the same sensations. If you need to give a speech, imagine how the audience will look sitting in front of you.

Take stock this weekend of the images with which you display yourself. Since the self-image comprises the visual, conceptual projection of self-esteem (clothes, auto, home, garage, closets, dresser drawers, desk, photos, lawn, garden), make a priority list to get rid of all the clutter and sharpen up the expressions of your life.

Go for a private walk and recall your childhood play. What did you love to do as a child? What were you good at? Which classes did you enjoy most throughout your school years? If it weren't for time, money or circumstance, what would you be doing with most of your days and nights? Dust off and reactivate your creativity.

What Every Woman Needs to Know

"What you see is who you'll be." The mind can't distinguish between what is real and what is vividly imagined. It stores as "truth" those images that are emotionally charged and repeated often.

What Every Man Needs to Understand

In order to help the woman in your life become more successful, reinforce her positive images of the future, and listen and nuture her when those images get blurred and rained on in the impatient, impersonal marketplace.

Chapter 8

•

Design Your Future

The theme of this chapter is self-direction, one of the most important characteristics of any achiever. Self-direction teaches you how to design your future and enjoy long-term success. It also guides you as you learn how to set meaningful goals and priorities.

• • •

Denis: Self-direction is the action plan that all winners in life use to turn imagination into reality, fantasy into fact, and dreams into actual goals. Self-direction is the power of purpose which sets successful people apart from the rest of humanity. Every winner we've ever met knows where he or she is going on a day-by-day basis, because winners are goal- and role-oriented.

They have a game plan for life. They're self-directed on their own road to self-fulfillment. A good definition of success is the progressive realization of goals that are worthwhile to you, as well as to other people.

Winners use positive self-direction to strengthen the dedication they need to follow through with their goals and achieve them, despite the setbacks and disappointments along the way.

Let's repeat our definition of success: *Success is the progressive, day-by-day realization of goals that are worthwhile to you, as well as to other people.*

That's true for all of us. We set a goal. The message is sent to our internal self-motivational system, which constantly monitors our self-talk and feedback about the goal. It also adjusts its self-image settings and starts making the necessary decisions to propel us into action to reach the goal.

Only five percent of the population will ever write down anything they want except groceries, appointments or incidentals. And only five percent of the population, usually that same five percent, will ever reach retirement age without depending on the government or someone else for their survival needs. Most people work to get through the week with enough extra money to spend on the weekend. But winners have specific goals.

• • •

A Clear and Focused Vision

Many hope they will get lucky and have opportunity knock, as in Publisher's Sweepstakes, with Ed McMahon and Dick Clark at the door with a big check. It's called the Lotto syndrome.

The goal needs to be clear, defined, and without any fuzzy edges. It's not enough just to say, "I want to be rich," or "I want a better job," or "I'd like to live someplace warm." If your subconscious is programmed with vague, random thoughts, you will get vague, random results. Let's turn those goals into something more definitive so you have the opportunity to achieve them.

Instead of "I want to be rich," name the exact amount of income every year that would make you happy. Instead of "I want a better job," spell out the exact position you want, the type of company you want it to be in, the salary you want to receive, and the time it's going to take you to get it. The more specific you can be about the duties you'd perform and even the types of people you'd be working with, the better chance you'll have of realizing your goal.

Instead of "I want to live someplace warm," get out a map and put a pin on the locale where you'd like to live. Say you want to live in Phoenix, Arizona. Write to the Chamber of Commerce in Phoenix and ask them to send you information on the city. Cut pictures out of magazines. Buy a poster of Camelback Mountain to hang on your wall. Subscribe to the local magazine and newspaper. If you surround yourself with visible reminders of what you want, you'll have it very quickly.

• • •

Deborah: After achieving my "wildest dream," I realized the significance of setting and visualizing specific goals. I learned that the greater the detail, the greater the chance of it happening just the way you wanted. The power is in being a proactive participant and cocreator of your destiny. I don't wait anymore to see what the future will bring—I design it.

As I was nearing completion of my doctoral studies, I wanted to explore different artistic mediums to express the insights I had gained over the years. It was important to me to find a living environment that would nourish and call forth my creative potential. To bring this new dimension of my life into existence, I knew I must focus my vision.

About this time, I had set foot in my dream house. In delivering a copy of my resume and bio to a speaker's booking agent who ran her business out of her home, I knew instantly this was the house I wanted to live in. Not just another house like it, but this very one. With a magnificent view of a lake, mountains and trees from every window, I was immediately put in touch with a deeper part of myself. The surrounding yard was a tiered hillside with gardens, shade trees, and a natural alcove of stone and rock formations. Redwood decks provided a place to share this world with friends and family. I saw myself here, creating the real work of my life.

I wrote down specific goals for myself and the exact activities I would accomplish each day while living in my dream house. I caught a glimpse of my ideal world. A realtor I had contacted informed me that I would be waiting a long time before something came available, but offered to let me know if and when it did. In my journal I designed the floor plan of my new house, complete with sketches and drawings of how I would decorate each room. In more detail, I planned out my office and studio space and even named some of the projects I would create in them. At night I had recurring dreams searching for a house to call my home. This went on for two years. Then one night I dreamed of a ritual or gathering in what appeared to be the booking agent's home—which was now being turned over to me.

One week later, I got a call from the realtor. He had a house to show me by the lake. As I wrote down the address, I felt a tingling sensation run through my body and recognized instantly that it was the house of my dreams.

I am now writing you these words from my desk, looking out onto a view that somehow we share. I know your own dreams and visions are awaiting your attention, ready to merge your future with your present direction.

●   ●   ●

Another goal-setting problem encountered by many people is fixating on an unrealistic goal that's too far out of sight. If you're thirty-five and your goal is to retire as a millionaire at 60, you're likely going to forget about it until you're 59 and then frantically begin buying lottery tickets.

Design Your Future

There's nothing wrong with wanting to retire wealthy, but you need to break the unattainable goal into smaller, more manageable goals. Get out your calculator and figure out the income you'll need every year to hit your target. Unless it has an immediate goal to focus on, the human system will wander aimlessly until it self-destructs with meaningless, escape-oriented, time-killing activities.

Next, narrow that manageable goal down to the next five years. Keep narrowing until you have a goal that can be managed within a few months or less. For instance, let's say you want to have $1,200 in your savings account at the end of the next six months. That means you need to put away $200 a month, or $50 a week. Now you have a goal that's achievable, a budget, and you're on your way to your ultimate goal, which isn't so far away anymore.

• • •

Denis: Perhaps more than anyone else, my former professor—the late Dr. Viktor Frankl—has given clarity to the human need for purpose. Dr. Frankl was a psychiatrist in Vienna at the outbreak of World War II and survived the Nazi concentration camps. His superb book, *Man's Search for Meaning*, which has been quoted by virtually every motivational speaker and self-help author, was written after he had endured three years of horror at Auschwitz and Dachau. We highly recommend that you read it, if you haven't already, along with *The Diary of Anne Frank.*

Frankl saw himself and his comrades stripped of literally everything—their families, professions, clothing, health, and even dignity. Existing in unspeakable circumstances, he studied the behavior of both captors and captives with a curious detachment. He saw how, faced with the identical situation, one individual degenerated while another attained virtual sainthood. Those prisoners who had no reason for staying alive, died quickly and easily.

However, the people who were able to survive the terrible trials of starvation and torture did so because they had a purpose for their existence. The one in twenty who survived the camps were, almost without exception, individuals who'd made themselves accountable to life. And that's the secret. There was something they wanted to do, a loved one they had to get back to, or a goal they had to achieve. In some instances, the goal was only to remember the faces of their captors so justice would one day be served, but that was enough. Others believed the Allies were coming in six months; this time frame gave them hope to hold on to and kept them alive.

When the prisoners would tell Dr. Frankl they no longer expected anything from life, he would argue strongly that they had it backward. Life was expecting something of them. Life asks of every one of us a contribution, and it's up to us to discover what that contribution will be. Life's not accountable to us—we're accountable to life.

People who are in transition, or those who're just trying to find themselves, can be intimidated, brainwashed, or seduced by skilled manipulators or fanatics who know that without a purpose you're an easy mark. They quickly buy into someone else's belief system, and it doesn't matter whether that belief system is good or bad, healthy or nonhealthy. As my friend and colleague Dr. Robert Schuller says, "If you don't stand for something, you'll fall for anything."

That's why internalized spiritual convictions, morals, and goals are so important. If you know where you're going, you'll get there. If you don't know where you're going, you'll end up on the road to nowhere.

• • •

Dedication in the Face of Challenge and Adversity

Vanity Fair magazine published an article by Gail Sheehy about Elizabeth Dole, who was serving as President of the American Red Cross at the time her husband, Bob, was running for President. The article quoted Elizabeth's high school math teacher, Miss Nicholson, who said, "Liddy has never failed to be prepared—it was true then, it's still true now."

In her own words, Liddy Dole sums up her personal success this way: "Self-improvement was a measure of personal growth. It was also a way to satisfy my goal-oriented parents." Today, when asked how she can accomplish so much, she says: "You look for five or six things where you can really make a difference and you go for it—put the blinders on and go."

Elizabeth Dole knows the meaning of dedication to her purpose, no matter what challenges she has to face.

• • •

Dayna: Here is an inspirational poem I have presented many times from the stage. It examines a woman's sense of purpose in life as she begins to set her goals and design her future.

Before you read this poem, think about the reflection you see when you look into a mirror. Do you see the child of your past? The person you are today? Or can you see the person that you are becoming? Well, maybe tomorrow, when you get up in the morning and look into your mirror, you can say:

Free to Be Me

Mirror, Mirror on my wall,
What's the meaning of it all?
Is there something more to life,
Than to be a loving wife?
Yes, I'll love my children dearly,

163

But they'll grow up and come by yearly.
Dare I yearn for something more,
Than to cook and wax the floor?
What about the needs I feel?
Are my dreams considered real?
What about an education and
A voice to shape our nation?
I've got a body and a soul,
I've got a mind, I've got a goal.
I want to learn, I want to teach,
I want to earn, I want to reach.
I want to fly from my cocoon and
Put my footsteps on the moon.
I'm not angry or rebelling, but there's
Something strong, compelling.
I don't want to be a man,
I love the woman that I am.
I can give the world so much
With my special female touch.
Mirror, Mirror, on my wall
Help me help him hear my call.
All I ever hope to be is
Free—to be that person, Me.

—Denis Waitley

P.S. Isn't it interesting that this poem, though written by a man, my father, speaks so well the words that women want men to hear? Men, help us find our calling in life beyond the cocoon so that we can give more freely of ourselves and be who we were meant to be. We will all live happier, more fulfilling lives as a result.

• • •

Hurdle the Roadblocks

Most people's big goals become root-bound, as if they tried to stuff a redwood tree into a flowerpot. They never achieve more than bonsai tree proportions because their self-images are compacted and contorted by their limited horizons. They never grow to their true potential. Instead of looking at ways to make their dreams come true, they list reasons why they wouldn't work out in the first place.

Your positive response to the challenge of your life—or your dedication to your purpose—is what enables you to face up to adversity and disappointment. No one reaches her goal without hurdling a few roadblocks put in her path. Most of the great success stories include the problems, failures, and set-backs that had to be dealt with before there could be forward movement. As Dr. Joyce Brothers says, "The person interested in success has to learn to view failure as a healthy, inevitable part of the process of getting to the top."

When we came home from school discouraged about some disappointment we'd had, we were encouraged to "Forget about the consequences of failure. Failure is only a temporary change in direction to set you straight for your next success."

And the author of *Uncle Tom's Cabin*, Harriet Beecher Stowe, wrote this excellent advice: "When you get into a tight place and everything goes against you, till it seems as though you could not hang on a minute longer, never give up then, for that is just the place and time that the tide will turn."

Never Give Up—As Long As You Live

Never give up. That's the answer. Continue your single-focused dedication to your goal.

So many times, the stories we read about senior people who are still active and vital describe the jobs they go to every day. In San Francisco, a doorman was still on the job on Union Square when he was over one hundred years old. A woman in Chicago was sewing professional sports uniforms in her nineties.

Another woman nearing one hundred is a well-respected handicapper at the race track. None of them had the time to be sick. They were active, alert, vital people who knew that work was the most potent elixir in the medicine chest. Did they have failures and disappointments? Of course they did. You don't reach your nineties and more without losing most of your old friends and many family members.

Several of these seniors have outlived their children— and even their grandchildren. But every one of them is described as "feisty." They're aggressive with life. They don't let anything deter them from what they want to do.

While not in that very senior age group, Margaret Dixon is a prime example of how to keep vital and on-track. She's president of the powerful AARP (American Association of Retired Persons), the largest organization of its kind in the world, with more than 32 million members over the age of 50—and the baby-boomers are just beginning to join. Furthermore, she is the first African-American president of the group.

For Margaret Dixon, this is a second career, one that grew out of her volunteer activities. She spent 26 years teaching in the New York public schools, eight of them as the principal of a large Brooklyn elementary school.

She and her husband retired in 1980 to a lovely home overlooking a lake in South Carolina.

Margaret says, "We could watch the ducks take off and land, but watching ducks gets tiresome after a while." She had earned two master's degrees and a doctorate in education along the way, and she wasn't going to give up teaching.

Immediately they began volunteering to teach literacy and became active in other charitable work. In 1988 they moved to Maryland to be closer to their children. That's when Margaret became most active in AARP. She worked her way up through the ranks, and recently, at the age of 73, she was appointed for a six-year term as president of this huge organization. She's never been busier, and she's delighted. The one word that isn't in her vocabulary is "retirement." She's re-inspired, instead of retired.

Be the Guardian of Your Mind

We all have the potential and opportunity to be successful. It takes just as much energy and effort to lead a bad life as it does a good life, maybe even a little more.

What is the power within us, the driving mechanism, that moves us toward our dominant obsessions? We know that the self-image can't tell the difference between an event that really took place and one that was vividly imagined. We also have learned that once our self-image receives a message with enough frequency, that message will become a habitual, automatic response that we accept as part of us.

Yes, old habits are hard to change. Even when they are told, "If you don't stop doing it, you're going to die!" some people still can't find the power within to change. The good news is, you really don't have to bear down and struggle with change. All you really need to do is dominate your thoughts on goal-achieving, instead of tension-relieving concepts.

Here's why: The same part of your brain that controls your heartbeat, breathing, reflexes and focus, also controls your goals.

We've known and talked about it for decades, but only recently have we learned all it does and how marvelous it is. It is called the *reticular activating system*, where the word "reticular" means network, as in network of cells that acts as the guardian of your priorities.

This incredible network of cells performs the unique function of filtering incoming stimuli (sight, sound, smell, taste and touch) and determining which ones are going to make an impression in your mind. It decides, from moment to moment, what information is going to become part of your world.

How many people do you know who won't listen to reason? Do you have any friends or family members who say they want your help but continue on a failure track? Of course—you see them every day.

What they don't realize is that they have tuned their reticular activating systems to guard their minds against success by unconsciously seeking the negative inputs and problems they say they are trying to avoid. By considering so often the possibilities of failure, their brains have been set to operate as failure-seeking guided missiles!

The reticular activating system filters out the unimportant stimuli and focuses on what is important at the moment. The sound of a crying child, a siren, or an unusual noise would cause you to pay less attention to listening to a tape, and direct your awareness to the urgent sound you heard.

Once you have made the distinction that a certain value, thought, idea, sound, picture, income, or level of fitness is significant to you, your reticular is alerted. It immediately transmits any information regarding this significant item into your consciousness, both from your memory and the environment.

A friend told us of a woman who recently bought a golden retriever, and she remarked to him that the advertisers are beginning to use golden retrievers in magazine and television ads, all of a sudden. He didn't want to burst her bubble of pride, but noted to himself that golden retrievers have been the most photographed and advertised dogs in America for over 30 years!

Have you ever bought a new car that the dealer said was rare and special as far as color and features, with very few in stock in the same county? Then how come so many similar models appear out of nowhere on the freeways and surface streets? It's as if all the smart people in the world had the same idea and taste as you. Well, they really didn't. It's just that once you value or fear something, your reticular goes to work and keeps on the alert for what you want and what you don't want, and it gives the same importance to your fears and goals.

The beautiful feature about the reticular activating system is that you can program it to be on the alert for success-related inputs, called images of achievement. It will wake you up in the morning without an alarm clock. It will take you for a brisk walk in the morning three times a week.

If you have a goal and are capable of weighing 120 pounds, without being anorexic, it will be on the lookout for ways to get you there. It will pass you by the chocolate cake in favor of the fresh fruit at the buffet table. But if you're always talking about how overweight you are, it will reinforce that condition.

If you are seeking more financial rewards, it will be extremely sensitive to any financially oriented data, both in your long-term memory and in the media, that could help you.

Be mindful of what you give importance to in your thinking and in your conversations with others. Your reticular activating system will turn your dominant thoughts into images of achievement or images of bereavement. It's your call.

• • •

The Five Powers of Purpose

Denis: There are five principles for structuring images of achievement for each of your goals, which we call The Five Powers of Purpose.

Power One is the Power of the Positive. Your goal statements must be stated in the positive, or you might achieve the reverse of what you really want. Forget about "not being late," "not being fat," and "not being broke or financially burdened." Focus on "being an on-time person," "lean and fit," and "saving 10 percent of your income each month."

Power Two is the Power of the Present. As we've repeated before, your goals must be stated in the present tense to be effective because your long-term memory stores everything in real time, such as breathing, heartbeat, and reflexes. It will dismiss into working memory things you want to do in the future, and those will be discarded soon if they are not given the priority of the here and now.

Power Three is the Power of Personal Goals. Make certain the goals you have are your own, not those of other significant adults in your life. No goal set for you by others will ever be sought with the same commitment as one you set for yourself.

Ask yourself, "What does being successful really mean to me? How will my life be improved by my success? What are the tradeoffs?" In other words, "What will I sacrifice or give up by accomplishing my goals—and am I willing to pay the price? How will other people benefit from my success? Who can I count on for support?"

Power Four is the Power of Precision. Make your goals specific and precise. The mind doesn't relate or respond to vague ideas. Would you ever dream of sending a carrier pigeon with the instructions, "Deliver this to my cousin Heidi"? Would you send your children to the store and say, "Get some good food for the rest of the month"? You may, but you'd be foolish without giving more explicit instructions. Many people say they want good health, but can't define it. They want enough money but have no idea how much is enough. We all want positive relationships, but do we stop to consider exactly what behaviors are important to us? Be specific about your goals.

Power Five is the Power of the Possible. Your goals need to be just out of your current reach, but not out of sight. It is vitally important to use an incremental approach to success. By setting lower level goals, ones that are relatively easy to accomplish, it's easier to make corrections when you get off target. The achievement of step-by-step goals also builds confidence. I co-authored a book called *Quantum Fitness,* while I was Chairman of Psychology for the U.S. Olympic Committee, that dealt with stair-stepping performance goals. I used an individual's resting heart rate as an example. Let's say your resting pulse is a bit high, in the 80s. You aspire to bring it down into the "excellence" range of 60 to 70, but that's a long-term goal. Your first step is to bring it under 80 through a nutrition and exercise program. When you wake up and find a pulse rate of 79 in a few weeks, celebrate. Go to a play or concert. Treat yourself to a new hairstyle or facial. Rejoice in small victories.

Then set your sights on a resting pulse of 75. Think of all those celebrations on your way down to the 60-something beats per minute. The point is to get a baseline of what is possible and experience success over and over again, so that winning becomes as much of a reflex as brushing your teeth or driving your car.

● ● ●

Achievers have lifetime goals that are different from their material goals. They ask themselves, "What do I stand for?" "What would I defend with my life?" "What would I want people to say about me after I'm gone?"

After they've clearly set their lifetime goals, they begin to set their "as soon as possible" goals. There aren't any time limits on these. These are the character, attitude, and behavior goals they don't dare put off any longer. If you put a time limit or a date on them, you may not reach them as quickly as you'd like. These are the short-term goals with long-term consequences—to be more charitable, to learn tolerance, to reach out a helping hand to someone less fortunate, and so on.

And most of all, achievers know that the most important time frames in life are the groups of minutes in every day, because most people waste most of their waking hours, every day, going through the motions, chatting idly, shuffling papers, putting off decisions, reacting, and majoring in minors. Since they have failed to plan, naturally, they're planning to fail by default.

Have you ever noticed that corporations and institutions have clearly defined plans, but only the top achievers in life have any kind of game plan for their own personal lives? Most of us spend more time planning a party, studying the newspaper, or making a Christmas list than we do charting the direction we want our lives to take.

Successful people set their daily goals the afternoon or evening before. They put down a list on paper in a priority sequence of the major things they'll do tomorrow. And they select priorities that lead toward the achievement of their most important current goal.

There's an old story about Dame Myra Hess, the concert pianist. After a recital at Carnegie Hall, a fan came up to her and said, "I'd give anything to play the way you do."

Dame Myra looked at her and replied, "I don't think so—or you already would play that way."

In other words, everything we accomplish exacts a price, whether it's giving up vacations to pay for extra schooling, or missing out on time with friends to practice the piano, or giving up a movie to spend time in the gym.

"Gameplan for Happiness" Journal Exercise

In your journal, write down what would give you the most fulfillment out of your work and your life. Be specific. The more defined, the better the aim and focus. At the top of the page, write the words: "My Goal Is to Be Happy." Underneath, write down what will make you happy.

If you want to make a lot of money, how much money over what time period? If you want to be famous, how are you going to do it? What are you going to excel in?

If you'd like to be president of the company, list the career steps you're going to have to take as you climb the ladder. Do you want to own your own business? By what date? In what field? And with how much capital required to start? Where will you get it?

Do you want financial security? Write down the dollar amount you want to have and the age you want to be when you get it.

Do you want more time for yourself? How do you plan to gain the hours, and what are the trade-offs you're going to have to make? How will it affect your family?

On another page, write down what you are willing to do to make yourself happy. Work extra hours? Get another degree? Lose twenty pounds? Apologize to a friend? Learn to speak Spanish?

Whatever it is, write it down. Where it makes sense, write down a game plan for achieving each of them. Factor

173

in the obstacles you may encounter, and think about how you'll go around them. Make the list as personal and meaningful to you as possible.

And it's vital that you share your goals only with other positive goal setters and supportive coaches. Misery is like a weed, always looking for a fertile patch of ground. Never share a goal with someone who's likely to flood your garden of dreams and rain on your parade with a downpour of negative reactions.

Chart Your Life's Course

So get behind the helm of your life, plan your work on a daily basis, and go forward one day at a time. See yourself achieving your goals, one by one. Remember that top achievers usually do one thing well at a time, and they don't stop until they achieve it. At this moment, you're nothing more than the sum total of all your thoughts and actions since you were a child. Similarly, who you'll be next year, five years from now, and throughout your lifetime hinges on what you think about from this moment forward.

We've all experienced how yesterday's pipe dreams have become today's necessities. Remember when there wasn't any e-mail, voice mail, fax machines, or home pages on the World Wide Web? Yet they're all part of our everyday experience today.

The 97-year old delegate to the national presidential convention was delighted to have spent an hour on the Internet with one of the cable news stations. How could anyone have predicted that in 1903 when she was born?

How can anyone but you see the achievements you have in store between now and the year 2020? What you see is who you'll be.

● ● ●

The Wheel of Fortune

Denis: In order to enlist the support of our associates, family, and friends in achieving our goals, we first must define them. Just by beginning to identify specifically what we want in life, the accomplishment is half done. Most people look at life like a TV game show in which you spin the wheel, try your luck, and win some expensive prizes or go home empty-handed. I'd like to introduce you to a different kind of "Wheel of Fortune." With this wheel, you can plan ahead to tilt the odds of winning in your favor from the start. If you understand the basics and follow the steps, you can win by design.

As we begin, let's examine a few relevant terms and definitions:

Luck: Laboring Under Correct Knowledge.

Once we know what we want to do and start preparing and doing it, we begin to have good luck.

Fear: False Education Appearing Real.

As we learned earlier, most of what we fear is imaginary, has already happened, is easy to solve once defined, or is beyond our control.

Procrastination: Hesitation caused by the fear of results, which can as often be the fear of success as the fear of failure.

Goals: Specific, action-oriented targets that can be defined, discussed, visualized, and committed to writing. Goals should be set just out of your current reach, but not out of sight.

Dreams: Daydreams are goals in the formative stages. Night dreams, normally, are subconscious episodes that help us resolve our emotional conflicts.

Dominant thoughts: Goals or obsessions that drive your daily life and priorities.

Self-talk: The silent conversations you have with yourself every minute about your life. Self-talk is also the conversation you have with other people about yourself and your goals.

Rules of the game: There is only one rule: Your Wheel of Fortune is not a game of chance, it is a game of choice. You will spend your life by the choices you make. There are no timeouts, no substitutions, and the clock is always running.

Warm-up exercises: Before we spin the wheel for real, let's get our brains limbered up with a few mind-stretching exercises. Answer "yes" or "no" to the following questions:

_____ Do I complete the projects I begin?
_____ Do I rehearse my goals in my imagination?
_____ Do I have a number of bad habits I can't seem to break?
_____ Do I have the same daydreams over and over about my success in a given field?
_____ Do I usually talk and think about my goals in a positive way?
_____ Do I know where I'm going in my life?

Next, let's use our imaginations to think of something enjoyable we want to do. If your dreams came true, what would your life be like? Dream a little by completing these sentences:

One goal I really want is _____
If I had a great deal of money I would _____
I would like to be the kind of person who _____
A place I would like to visit is _____
My life would be better if _____
If I had the time I would _____
If I could start over I would _____

Design Your Future

As the final warm-up exercise, honestly consider the major roadblocks that have been holding you back from rolling your Wheel of Fortune down the road of life with greater speed and to more destinations. The following are various obstacles people say prevent them most from getting what they want out of life. Check the ones you feel have restricted or limited you:

- insufficient education
- in with the wrong crowd
- insufficient capital
- slow learning
- bad economic times
- bad credit rating
- inflation
- wrong party in power
- government
- alcohol, drugs, etc.
- uncooperative spouse
- wrong horoscope
- negative family upbringing
- out of step with the times
- chose the wrong profession
- always pick the wrong job
- too many dependents
- unresponsive boss
- physically not attractive
- limited family support
- discrimination
- economically depressed city
- promotion policies
- chose obsolete industry.

I believe that you would not be this far into this book if you were not a winning individual. People with low self-esteem, who are poorly motivated, rarely (if ever) read books that are designed to help them. They concentrate strictly on "escape" pastimes. This book is a journey to discover self, rather than escape from self.

The reason I mention this is that I doubt that you checked a large number of items under the major roadblocks that have prevented you from reaching your goals in life.

I think you and I can be honest with ourselves. Perhaps you did not get the education you wanted. Your organization may not recognize your outstanding abilities. Your spouse's primary objective may seem to be keeping you humble.

Whatever the problem, you and I know that you are responsible for the eventual outcome of your life. You have been given the greatest power in the world—the power to choose. You understand that the goals and decisions you have chosen in the past have brought you to your present circumstances. You also realize that your future will be determined, in large measure, by the goals you have set for yourself that guide your daily decisions. You and I both know that our self-esteem, creative imagination, and feeling of responsibility for causing our own effects are the major roadblocks or green lights on our roads of life. Let's keep these ideas in mind as we consider how to play the Wheel of Fortune.

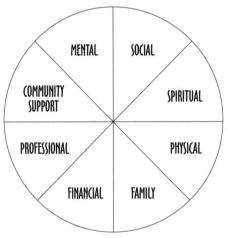

Looking at the Wheel of Fortune illustration, there are eight segments in the Wheel. For each of the eight segments, I have listed a few goal-starter ideas from which you can begin to construct your own Wheel of Fortune. I know that you may be way ahead of this fundamental approach to goal setting, but even if you are, play along with me as a means of checking your own progress.

• • •

Select one of the starter ideas I have listed for each of the eight segments, or pick a specific idea that you have been working on. Select something you are going to accomplish by the end of this year, and set yourself a deadline for completing it.

GOAL STARTER IDEAS

Select one of the ideas below or list one of your own:

PHYSICAL
Sports Skill (male)
Different Weight
(*female*)
Eating Right
Exercise Schedule

Example
I will take golf or tennis lessons
I'm going to weigh 125 pounds

When? By December 1st

FAMILY
Relationship Parents

Example
Call my mother more often
When? Now and twice a month
        hereafter.

COMMUNITY SUPPORT _____When? _____
Service organizations
Volunteer work
Civic office or committees
Walk- or bike-a-thons

MENTAL _____When? _____
Read nonfiction books
Self-improvement courses
Improve vocabulary
Own personal computer

SOCIAL   _____When? _____
Make new friends
Dress and look my best
Club activities
New recreational pursuits

SPIRITUAL   _____When? _____
Attend regular religious services
Read religious publications
More time in meditation and prayer
More effort loving and serving others

How to Mine Your "Goal Mind"

Now that you have selected eight goal starters from the Wheel of Fortune, it is time to pick up where most seminars leave off. Remember at the beginning of this chapter, when we learned that the reason most people fail to achieve their goals in life is that they never set them in the first place? I am convinced this next step is extremely important in internalizing even the most basic of your goals.

By reading these "self-talk" statements several times daily or listening to the goal statements as recorded by your own voice, as if you had already achieved them, you can accelerate the internalization of your goals. Your self-image cannot distinguish between reality and something vividly imagined. The habit of repeatedly reinforcing your own goals as if they were in the present tense introduces visual, emotional and verbal suggestions to your creative imagination at the subconscious level. These suggestions, if repeated in a relaxed environment with frequency, will tend to override your previous habit patterns with a new game plan that you have designed for success.

Design Your Future

To steer your Wheel of Fortune down a yellow brick road and convert your "goal mind" into a "gold mine," take the eight goal starters that you selected in each category and define them, specifically, in one sentence, below:

Dimension	Goal	When
1. Physical	Weigh 125 pounds and tone my muscles	By Dec. 1
2. Family	_____	_____
	_____	
3. Financial	_____	_____
	_____	

Dimension	Goal	When
4. Professional	_____	_____
	_____	
5. Community	_____	_____
	_____	
6. Mental	_____	_____
	_____	
7. Social	_____	_____
	_____	
8. Spiritual	_____	_____
	_____	

It is not unusual for successful individuals to be working on four or five goals in each of the eight categories, at the same time. I know many top managers and leaders in every field who review several goals each day and listen to audio cassette recordings in their own voice of those goals as they travel to and from their place of business. Interestingly enough, these same individuals seem to be the happiest, best adjusted, best married, best parents, and most financially secure people I have ever met. They know where they want to go in life, and they are on the right road.

Now that you have one goal in each of the eight categories, defined as to what it is and when you plan to accomplish it, write each of these goals in your journal as if it has already been reached.

- Use the pronoun "I," and use:
- Present tense verbs (am enjoying, am doing, etc.)
- Action modifiers (easily, regularly)
- Emotion words (enthusiastically, happily)
- Goal (present tense)

Examples:

Physical Goal (female)—"I enjoy weighing 125 pounds and feeling healthy and energetic."

Physical Goal (male)—"I weigh a trim, athletic 165 pounds and enjoy exercising every day."

As you write these "self-talk" statements in your journal, you should use some subtle refinements in the sentence construction; this can spell the difference between success and failure in your internalization of the goal suggestions. In working with astronauts, Olympic athletes, and clinical psychololgists engaged in behavior modification, I have found the following principles to work best for positive statements:

1. *Always use personal pronouns.* Words such as "I," "my," "mine" and "me" will personalize your statements and make them easier to affirm and assimilate.

Ineffective: "Jogging is good exercise."

Effective: "I enjoy jogging three miles every day."

2. Keep your self-talk in the present tense. Referring to the past or future dilutes the impact or may be counterproductive to the internalization of your goals.

Ineffective: "Someday I'll go to Hawaii."

Effective: "I love the surf and sand in Maui."

3. Keep your goal statements short and concise (four to five seconds long).

Ineffective: "Now that I have saved $5,000, I may go into business for myself, and I hope to succeed."

Effective: "My business is properly capitalized with the five thousand dollars I put into it."

4. Direct your self-talk toward what you desire, instead of trying to come away from what you don't want.

Your mind can't concentrate on the reverse of an idea. If you try to tell yourself not to repeat mistakes, your mind will reinforce the mistake. You want to focus your current dominant thought on your desires, not your dislikes.

Ineffective: "I can quit smoking."
"I will lose 20 pounds."
"I am not late any more."
"I don't yell at the children."
"I won't double-fault my tennis serves."

Effective: "I am in control of my habits."
"I weigh a slim, trim 125 pounds."
"I arrive early for appointments."
"I am patient and loving with my kids."
"I'll get the first serve in play."

5. Keep your self-talk noncompetitive, rather than comparing yourself with others.

Ineffective: "I will become a starter on the team before he or she does."

Effective: "I am starting on the team and doing the job well."

6. In writing your statements, strive for improvement over your current status. Don't strive for perfection.

Ineffective: "I'm the best sales executive in the company, making the most money."

Effective: "Im doing my best this year, producing twenty percent more than last year."

Once you have correctly written a goal statement in your journal for each of the eight categories in the Wheel of Fortune, get in the habit of carrying them with you as often as possible. Read the statements in the morning at the beginning of your normal routine, look them over during the day, and read them again before you retire at night. Visualize yourself having already reached each goal. Allow yourself to actually feel the pride of doing well.

The Awesome Power of Suggestion

I'm impressed with the methods used by Russia, Germany, and Bulgaria in training their Olympic athletes to gain high performance through suggestopedic learning. They instruct an athlete to listen to classical music while at the same time a goal tape, recorded in the athlete's own voice, is softly playing. The individual enjoys and focuses on the music, while the goal statements become a subliminal, background sound. The goals, however, should be audible and recognizable.

The rhythmic beat of the slow classical music appears to provide a relaxation mode for the brain, making it most susceptible to visual and audio suggestion and releasing the dominance of the left hemisphere to allow the right hemisphere to respond to the goal affirmations. Since the right hemisphere seems to house most of our negative, subconscious feelings about ourselves, our repeated goal statements may literally change the way we view ourselves and thus alter the direction of our lives.

Don't let the technique of affirmation and simulation give you the false impression that we are brainwashing ourselves or lying to ourselves. What I am suggesting is the opposite from brainwashing, or kidding ourselves. We are, unwittingly, being brainwashed and lied to every day of the week, day and night. The programs we watch, the magazines we read, the inputs we listen to, the people we talk to—all of these are giving us a sensationalized, dramatized perception of what is happening in the world. I perceive most of society's inputs as negative. Isn't it time that you and I concentrated on information designed for our success rather than our frustration? Isn't it time we switched from washing our minds with "soaps" to programming our minds with goals?

The mind is goal-seeking by design. Successful individuals have game plans and purposes that are clearly defined and to which they constantly refer. They know where they are going every day, every month, and every year. Things don't just happen in their lives. They make life happen for themselves and their loved ones. They know the difference between goal-achieving actions and activities that are just tension-relieving.

Purpose is the engine that powers our lives. Everyone has purpose. For some it is to eat; for others it is to get through the day. For many Americans it is to make it to Friday so they can celebrate "TGIF" at the local watering hole. For you and me, personal growth, contribution, creative expression, loving relationships, and spiritual harmony are the common goals that make us try to be uncommon people. Specific, written goals are the tools which make purpose achievable. Since the mind is a biocomputer, it needs definitive instructions and directions. The reason most people don't reach their goals is that they don't define them, learn about them, or ever seriously consider them as believable or achievable.

While the others watch in the viewing audience, you and I will grab our Wheel of Fortune and take command. We can tell the others where we are going, approximately how long it will take, why we are going, what we plan to do along the way, and who will be sharing the adventure with us. You and I live our lives—on purpose!

Ten Action Steps toward Your Goals

1. Set short-range goals that build toward your long-range purpose. It is much more effective to establish goals for one month, six months, or one year, than to project too far into the future. Specific time limits are important measuring devices.

2. Set goals that are just out of reach, but not out of sight. It is critically important to use an incremental approach to success. By setting lower-level goals, ones that are relatively easy to accomplish, it is easier to make corrections when you get off target. The achievement of step-by-step goals also builds your confidence.

3. Get group reinforcement by surrounding yourself with motivated individuals interested in the same achievement. Also, review your goals with experts. Get counsel from people with proven track records of success.

4. Establish a reward or ceremony in advance, so that you will have something specific to celebrate upon the accomplishment of each of your goals. It may be a trip, a family dinner, some special recreation, new clothing, or a personal item.

5. Try a different kind of New Year's celebration. Put your goals for this year in an envelope. Encourage your family members to do the same. On New Year's Eve or New

Year's Day, open the envelopes and see how well you did in accomplishing what you set out to do. It is a fantastic way to end another great year. Then set your goals for the new year.

6. Use a desktop or briefcase calendar to set your goals for next month. What will you do, where will you go, and with whom will you communicate?

7. Use a pocket, week-at-a-glance calendar to set your activities for next week that will take you step-by-step toward your monthly and annual goals.

8. Use an 8 1/2 x 11 lined folio pad or journal to set the most important goals of all your daily priorities. At the close of each day, set your priorities for tomorrow. Review your list at the beginning of each new day, before you make your first call or appointment. Check off each item as it is accomplished, and carry over those priorities not completed into the following day's agenda.

9. Don't share your goals with negative people or cynics. Share your goals with people who really care about you and want to help you. And make certain you take the advice of winners. Remember, misery loves company. Some people would just as soon you stayed in the same rut along with them!

10. Don't depend upon the government for your long-range financial security. Pay yourself each month by putting a sum of money in a savings account for your future, as if you were paying your house payment. You are your best Social Security.

"Questions about Your Purpose" Journal Exercise

1. What is one of your personal goals this month? What will you do today that contributes to that goal?

2. What is one of your professional goals this month? Have you shared this goal with anyone who can reinforce your purpose?

3. Do you have a game plan for the year?

4. Do you have physical fitness goals established? Check to see that they are stated in specific language.

5. Will you be able to live in later years without worrying about Social Security? Have you decided how much you will put away in savings each month?

6. What are you going to do tomorrow? Will you carry over the items that you didn't get to today, and make them tomorrow's goals?

In the next chapter, we'll learn how to convert your goals into winning habits with dedication and self-discipline.

What Every Woman Needs to Know

Focus always precedes success. Specificity is the key. Generalization leads to procrastination and rationalization. "If you don't know where you're going, any old road will take you there!"

What Every Man Needs to Understand

Just because you assume you know exactly where you're going doesn't make you right. When you get lost, it's prudent to ask for directions. Using a map does not mean you are not "macho."

Chapter 9

———•———

Dedicate Your Mind

*E*arlier, we described the need for the characteristic of self-direction, which is specificity in goal setting in every area of our lives. Self-discipline converts goals into achievements because it is the combination of practice and persistence.

• • •

Denis: Self-discipline means paying the price of winning, and the theme of positive self-discipline is practice, practice, practice. Like the other qualities we've talked about, self-discipline is a habit that you must cultivate. Self-discipline dares you to wager on your own abilities. It's where the rubber meets the road.

All of the other winning characteristics in this program are absolutely worthless without self-discipline. You may accept yourself as talented. You may be confident of your abilities. You may be determined to become the first woman president. You may desire the office with a burning passion. You may expect to win the election. You may dream of living in the White House. But you'll never even go on a guided tour of the Rose Garden if you haven't cultivated within yourself a persistent self-discipline.

In theory, it would seem that all you have to do is tell yourself that you'd like a new self-image and memorize your goals, and then "zap," like a microwave oven, you're done.

The truth is there's a little more effort involved because you've probably spent most of your life operating under the old system. Every day your actions and reactions confirm and support your present self-image.

You constantly talk to yourself, at about 400 to 600 words a minute, maintaining and justifying "who you are" today. And this has been going on for years. We talked in an earlier chapter about the analogy of comparing our self-image with an ATM machine. It allows us to make deposits and withdrawals. We can transfer from one habit to another. We can find out what our balance is and review our past activities. Our inner ATM is a major "control room" for our habits.

Habits are the keys because they can start out innocently enough as an off-hand remark, or an ad in a magazine, or friendly hints, or personal experiments. Habits are very much like cobwebs. A cobweb seems flimsy and easily breakable—unless you're a fly that's been caught in it.

The power of habit is your greatest force for success. We all first make our habits. Then our habits make us. And it happens so subtly, over time, imperceptibly, quietly, beneath the notice of anyone. Habits are like submarines. They run silent and deep.

The chains of our habits are usually too small to be recognized until they're too strong to be broken. First we observe the behavior of relatives, friends, or role models. Then we imitate that behavior. Then we repeat and internalize the behavior, and the belief or act grows, layer upon layer.

● ● ●

One thing is certain, if we do not master our habits—our habits will master us. When you have the habit of self-discipline, then you'll find you also have the habit of achieving, like Dr. Laura.

Dr. Laura Schlessinger has been heard every day on radio by millions of people across the United States for several years. She has the reputation for being tough but fair with her callers, trying to help but refusing to let them fall back into patterns of victimization and self-pity.

However, Dr. Laura has weathered a lot of storms on her own. Without missing a beat, she nursed her husband through a heart attack and six bypass surgeries, survived the loss of her house (which burned to the ground because of an electrical fire) and the damage to her new home from the Los Angeles earthquake.

In spite of this, she's written several best-selling books, is the very-involved mother of an adolescent son, and has a black belt in karate. Asked how she does it all, Dr. Laura said, "I just get into gear and take care of business." She's a perfect example of self-discipline in action, which she has used to develop the habits of success.

Embracing the Gift—Not the Guilt—in Life

We often hear self-discipline defined as doing without, and many people do practice it that way. Some enjoy denying themselves all pleasure in the name of self-discipline. They don't spend a penny they don't absolutely have to. They avoid entertainment and devote every extra minute to self-improvement activities. They never eat a food that isn't healthy. They work late, exercise early, and feel guilty if they start to find it fun.

• • •

Denis: That's not what we're advocating. Life is a gift given to us to be enjoyed. Self-discipline is not necessarily the sacrifice of doing without. Self-discipline is "doing within when you're doing without." Let's say that again: *Self-discipline is doing within when you're doing without.* You see, self-discipline is nothing more than mental practice. It's training your mind to control your body.

An old proverb says, "Habits are easier to abandon today than tomorrow." The reason is that, every day, the habit behavior becomes more and more ingrained into your subconscious, until changing becomes very difficult.

The impact of habits has been dramatic in our own family. My father died of lung cancer and liver disease when chain-smoking, after heavy drinking caught up with him and robbed him of the golden years of his life. My mother was 90 and healthy when we wrote this book, and she knows how much he has missed. By becoming a slave to his habits, he forfeited the opportunity to see his children achieve their lifelong goals, to know his grandchildren and great-grandchildren.

My dad saw success for his children, but not for himself. He was a caring coach for me, but not a very disciplined role model. As Mr. Goodwrench, the auto mechanic in the old television commercial, reminds us, "You can pay me now or pay me later." Sooner or later your good habits bear fruit, and your bad habits sow the seeds of destruction.

● ● ●

Go to your journal and look at the page where you wrote down the list of habits you want to change and the habits you want to replace them with. Keep going over this list every day. Too often, we write something down and consider it taken care of.

Instead, continue reminding yourself what you have to do to change your habits for the better. But don't just read the list, begin to do something to change your behavior. Look at what you're doing and examine the reasons why you're doing it.

Filling the Empty Spaces

In her book, *The Undefended Self*, Susan Thesenga says that many of our bad habits are the result of unmet needs for affection, companionship or communication.

As she puts it, "People do not want to feel their aching for contact and love. Instead, they turn to something that will distract their attention: TV, food, or whatever. All of these distractions can temporarily abate the hunger for satisfying relationships."

If your bad habits are filling in the empty spaces, then face this fact squarely so you can begin to replace them with healthy, satisfying activities. As this happens, expect to go through a kind of mourning period. If you've been a smoker for twenty years, for example, you will physically feel a loss when you stop smoking. If you're prepared for this reaction, it will be easier to work through.

But, as the writer Anatole France commented, "All changes, even the most longed for, have their melancholy, for what we leave behind us is a part of ourselves. We must die to one life before we can enter into another."

When we begin to deal with the attitudes and actions that bind us, we give ourselves permission to take control and to build new habit-patterns that help us perform up to our ultimate potential.

Repetition—Habit—Conviction—Action

There is a critical difference between knowing something and learning how to make it a part of our everyday game plan. The secret is repetition, repetition, repetition. Repetition creates habit. Habit becomes conviction. Conviction controls action.

Right now, in this instant, you are engaged in one of the best habits of all, that of reading information which will ben-

193

efit you rather than frustrate and defeat you. The repeated study of knowledge to help form positive self-management skills has helped thousands of individuals all over the world achieve their goals and become uncommonly successful.

Advertising executives on Madison Avenue bet their careers and their clients' enormous budgets on the fact that repeated messages cause subconscious decisions. Every Saturday morning, they teach our kids which brands of cereal they should eat, what kinds of shoes are cool, and which video games, CD's, software, footwear, and toys they should get their parents to buy.

It should come as no surprise that, after the body responds the same way to identical stimuli 25 or 30 times, a habit is formed. Think about it: only 25 or 30 repeats for a habit to be formed, and it becomes like a software program installed in the hard drive of our minds. We don' t think about it—we just run the program. While it seems more difficult to replace a bad habit with a good one, the development of good habits enjoys the same, precise mathematical formula. It depends on input, practice, and supporting environment.

Cornerstones of Change

There are four ideas that we call the four "Cornerstones of Change." Understanding these four concepts will help you understand the right way to develop healthy habits:

Cornerstone One: No one else can change you. You must first admit the need for change, give up any denial of your role in the problem, and take responsibility for changing yourself. You must also understand that you can't change anyone else, either. You can influence and inspire others as a mentor. But they, as individuals, are ultimately responsible for gaining new inputs, practicing them, and surrounding themselves with a team of positive supporters.

Cornerstone Two: Habits are not broken—they are replaced by layering new behavior patterns on top of the old ones, over time. Since many habits have been internalized for years, don't assume that three or four weeks of training will override the old destructive patterns.

To change any habit, including substance abuse, self-ridicule, eating disorders, and other destructive lifestyles, forget about the quick fixes. Give yourself about a year to internalize permanent change. Be patient. It took years of observation, imitation, and repetition for you to pick up and store your current habits.

Cornerstone Three: Practice makes permanent. A daily routine, adhered to over time, will become second-nature, like brushing your teeth or driving your car. Continue to practice your mistakes on the golf driving range, and you'll remain a high handicap duffer. Learn from a professional and then practice the correct swing with each club as demonstrated by the pro, and you'll become the pride of your foursome.

Practicing negative behaviors leads to a losing lifestyle. Practicing positive behaviors leads to a winning lifestyle. It is so obvious, it is often completely overlooked, especially by the entertainment and news media, who help form our basic opinions on how the world works.

You can't erase any thought, experience, or habit. You can only replace it by flooding your mind with the desired behavior. The more we try to suppress or forget about unwanted thoughts, the more likely we are to become preoccupied with them.

Psychologist Daniel M. Wegner and his colleagues told a group of college students not to think about white bears. He then asked them to dictate their ongoing thoughts into a tape recorder and ring a bell each time a white bear came to mind. Not thinking about white bears proved difficult for the students.

They rang the bell or mentioned the bear more than once a minute during a five-minute session. This proved why it is so difficult to get rid of unwanted attitudes. In trying not to think about a white bear, the researchers explain, we must first think about it.

The researchers repeated the experiment, but this time told another group of students to think about a red Volkswagen if they happened to think of a white bear. Using a single "substitute" thought worked. It helped the students avoid thinking of the dreaded white bear. When your worries or fears beg for attention, don't try to erase them from your mind. Replace them with thought of the rewards of success, which for you may be a red Ferrari (instead of a red Volkswagen), a satisfied client, or a goal achieved.

Cornerstone Four: Once you change a habit, stay away from the old destructive environment. The reason most criminals return to prison is that they make the mistake of returning to their old neighborhoods and their old friends when they are paroled the first time. No matter how much they have regretted their actions while in prison and want to go straight, they are easily dragged back into their old ways by exposure to a negative environment.

When dieters reach their desired weight, they usually go back to their former eating routines because their new behavior patterns haven't been imbedded long enough to make them strong enough to pass by the dessert section of the buffet.

If you want to stay optimistic and successful, you must hang out in success-related environments.

• • •

Denis: Here are six key points to ponder in reviewing and internalizing what we have just covered:

1. First, we make our habits. Then our habits make us.

2. The chains of our habits are too small to be felt until they're too strong to be broken.

3. Much of TV and entertainment is a growing ground for destructive behavior. Children's habits are a reflection of significant adult role models in their lives. They are unaware that habits are being formed.

4. Although most change comes from inner, core convictions, it is possible for external environments with a consistent flow of new, positive inputs to create new habits and lifestyles.

5. Many habit patterns give way to former destructive habit patterns because the individual attempts to become a "new person" in the same, old environment.

6. Habits don't discriminate. They are the masters of every failure, and the servants of every leader who has ever lived.

"Positive Habit Formation" Action Tips

Now here are some Action Tips for Positive Habit Formation:

1. Identify your bad habits. When, where, and why did you learn and develop them? Are you unconsciously imitating peers or negative role models? Do you use them to cover fear or feelings of inadequacy, in other words, emotions that would cause you to seek false comfort in tension-relieving instead of goal-achieving activities?

2. Learn what triggers your bad habits. Identifying your unwanted patterns makes replacing them easier, beginning with the triggers, which often are stress, criticism, guilt, or feelings of rejection. Identify the situations that cause you the most frustration and tension, and plan ways to avoid or to reduce them as much as possible.

3. List in your journal the benefits of a new habit that would replace the old one. Self-esteem, improved health, better relationships, a more rewarding career, etc.

4. Say farewell forever to excuses for mistakes and failures. Accept your imperfection when an old habit begs for attention. Instead of saying, "There I go again," replace that thought with, "Next time I'll be strong enough to do what's right."

5. Visualize yourself in the new habit patterns of a new, winning lifestyle. It takes many simulations and repetitions to spin new cobwebs on top of your old cables.

● ● ●

If you want to give up smoking, intentionally sit in non-smoking areas and request nonsmoking rooms and restaurant tables. Substitute breath mints or fat-free snacks when the craving reminds you to reach for a pack. Only a supportive, optimistic approach toward your habits will take you where you want to go.

Take Time to Revitalize

The beauty of visualization is that it requires nothing more complicated than your mind, a quiet space where you can relax completely, and a few moments of your time in solitude. Every visualization or meditation exercise suggests that you find a quiet place where you can be alone. Each of us needs time by ourselves for rest and revitalization.

Dr. Harriet B. Braiker says, "High-achieving women are imploded with demands, both external and internal, and lack the skills to filter them. These women complain that the first thing they sacrifice is their private time or private pleasures." Psychologists refer to what happens to us as "privacy deprivation syndrome." We become so stressed trying to meet all the demands of the people around us that we fall into bed exhausted at night.

We're unable to sleep well because we're worried about what the next day's going to bring. The cycle continues until, finally, the body takes over and we come down with the flu, a headache or worse. Whatever the symptoms, you can be certain it's our body's way of telling us to take a break, to give it a rest. There's never a reason for us to allow the world to be so overbearing that we can't take a few minutes a day for ourselves.

● ● ●

Deborah: During my corporate ladder climbing years, I was a full-fledged workaholic. Twelve to sixteen hour days were typical, and I rarely took time just for me. It finally reached a point, however, that my body began dictating my vacation (sick) days. Constant colds, headaches, breast lumps, and other physical ailments became more frequent, and I realized I needed time to step back, relax, and revitalize. I learned almost too late that if you don't dedicate your mind to nurturing your body and spirit, your life will be out of balance. Time for revitalizing should be scheduled into every self-discipline program.

As I had taken my work life to an extreme, I took my revitalization to an extreme as well. I heard about a special place, a retreat on top of a mountain in Taos, New Mexico. I knew I needed this experience of total seclusion to bring me back to my center.

I met the hermitage master, who took me to a cellar at the foot of the mountain where I chose root vegetables, apples, water, and matches for my six days. He led me halfway up the mountain, and carrying only my backpack, I walked the rest of the way on my own. When I reached the one-room cabin, tears welled up in my eyes. Here was my home in the wilderness, and I knew I would leave this place a different person than I was now.

For the first two hours, I was in agony of withdrawal from the comforts of the world: voicemail, telephones, television, radio, and junk food. Only me, the mountain, trees, wildlife, wind, and silence. When night fell, my only light was a kerosene lamp, my only heat a wood-burning stove. As I stoked the fire throughout the night to keep warm, I stoked the very cinders of my soul. I spent time reading the journal entries of all those who had stayed in this cabin before me and discovered we had all shared very similar experiences. I spent the days hiking and exploring the mountain and knew I would return to the world with a clearer mind and a new perspective on life.

Since that experience, I have been scheduling regular time to revitalize. I have carved out some time in each day that is mine alone. Though I don't need to fly to a mountain top or tropical island to rejuvenate, I have learned to create a sacred space within my own home in which to retreat and center myself. I encourage you to create your own special time and space. It can be one section of your home or backyard, or perhaps a special place out in nature within walking or driving distance. You deserve this gift to yourself. You will be enchanted by the dedication and discipline of your mind and spirit.

●　●　●

Dayna: In an era of incessant change and exploding information technology, it is vital that we take time to replenish our spirit and rekindle our relationships. As I tuck my children into bed each night, I take a moment to resolve conflicts, reinforce my unfailing support, and most of all, to tell them that I love them unconditionally.

My dad and step-mother, Susan, wrote this poem which I did not fully understand or appreciate until I became a parent.

Take A Moment

Take a moment to listen today to what
your children are trying to say.

Listen to them, whatever you do or
they won't be there to listen to you.

Listen to their problems, listen to their needs.

Praise their smallest triumphs, praise
their littlest deeds.

Tolerate their chatter, amplify their laughter.

Find out what's the matter, find out
what they're after.

If we tell our children all the bad in
them we see,

They'll grow up exactly how we
hoped they'd never be.

But if we tell our children we're so
proud to wear their name,

They'll grow up believing they can
win their full-life's game.

So tell them that you love them
every single night,

And as you tiptoe out, say, "Happy
dreams, sleep tight."

Turn off the light and turn around and
say, "Oh, by the way,

Regardless of our differences today,

Everything's all right, tomorrow's
looking bright."

Take a moment to listen today to what
the children are trying to say.

Listen to them, whatever you do, and
they'll be there to listen to you.

P.S. It is imperative that you men take precious moments to spend with your children and families. It is difficult to manage the pressures of making a living while trying to live a happy and productive life. Make sure you revitalize yourself every chance you get. I think it's typically more difficult for men to carve solitude into their lives, you're so busy managing, strategizing, directing, planning, and doing. When you finally take some time out for you, it is most likely in the company of your significant partner or buddies. Give yourself the gift of the present—private time alone to reflect, contemplate, dream—and just be!

● ● ●

"Solitary Pleasures" Journal Exercise

In your journal, make a list of the solitary pleasures that would make you happy.

One woman we know gets away from stress by going into the family room and working on a complicated jigsaw puzzle for while. There's always a puzzle spread out on the table, and she says it acts as an immediate tranquilizer. When she's concentrating on which piece goes where, she has no time to think about anything else. Another takes her dog for an extra mid-afternoon walk. Still another works on a large piece of needlepoint.

Dedicate Your Mind

Whatever your particular solitary pleasure is, allow enough time for it. Don't let radio, television, or cassette players intrude, unless you are listening to soothing orchestral music or nature sounds. Once you are alone, allow yourself to visualize how you would like your behavior to be.

Scientific research has confirmed our incredible ability to achieve any thought that's uppermost in our minds. Our brains instruct our bodies to carry out the actual performance as if it had been achieved before and is merely being repeated. One of the major reasons that many individuals fail to reach their goals is that they don't understand—or they're not willing—to exercise the determination and self-discipline, the mental strengthening of practicing "within" when they are "without."

When skater Kristi Yamaguchi won the gold medal in the Winter Olympics at Albertville, France, some years ago, she had posted an almost perfect score despite a fall during her performance. What made her so much better than the other competitors, despite the mistake? She would tell you it was visualization. From the time she was six years old, Kristi Yamaguchi had seen herself as an Olympic champion. The picture was so real in her mind that her body had no choice but to achieve it. Combine visualization with the self-discipline of an athlete, and you have a gold medal combination.

In addition to the pictures in your journal, put a picture of what you want on the mirror in the bathroom, inside your closet door, or on the dashboard of your car—anywhere that you'll be sure to see it several times a day. The picture will act like a trigger to your subconscious and precipitate the habit-changing behavior you need.

Successful people simulate and practice succeeding, so you need to discipline yourself to win. You practice right before you go to sleep at night, and you practice right after you wake up in the morning. You practice in the shower, while you're fixing dinner, and while you're driving to work. You practice whenever you have a few moments of free time because winning self-discipline is doing within when you are without.

● ● ●

Positive Self-Discipline Key Points

Denis: Here are the key points we want you to remember about Positive Self-Discipline:

First, visualize the habits and actions you want until they become as familiar as making coffee in the morning. Don't forget that every day we should take our cues from those who are masters of the art of visual and sensory simulation, such as athletes, pilots, and musicians. Imitation isn't only the sincerest form of flattery, it's also the best way to achieve what you want.

Second, understand that there's a winner's behavioral cycle. Our self-image determines our performance. No matter what we do, afterwards we instantaneously engage in self-talk with words, pictures, and emotions to confirm or to adjust our self-image about that particular action.

It's a victor's circle or vicious cycle that either takes us up or down. And the self-talk that we use after every performance determines whether the new self-image will reinforce the win or reinforce the loss.

After every performance—whether it's closing a sale, speaking in front of a group, communicating with your employees, playing golf or tennis, or interacting with family and friends—you must control your self-talk to reaffirm or elevate your positive self-image.

If you've performed well, your self-talk should be "that's more like the me I want to be." If you aren't pleased with what you've done, you say, "I perform better than that. The next time I'll do better." And then replay the action correctly in your imagination, envisioning it happening exactly how it should be done correctly.

Be careful at this point. It's easy to fall into the trap of replaying the action as you actually performed it, not as you wanted to perform it. When you see yourself making a mistake, that mistake becomes implanted in your subconscious.

It's as if you were went out to lunch with friends and all the way to the restaurant you said to yourself, "I won't eat the rolls. I won't eat the butter. And especially, I won't eat any dessert!" Remember the dangers of negative self-talk!

By saying "I won't eat the rolls," you've programmed your mind to do exactly what you didn't want to do. Of course, when you meet your friends, you immediately dive into the basket of rolls, spreading each one with lots of butter. And when dessert is offered, since everyone else is having something, you have something, too.

Back in your car, you think about what you did. Do you see yourself eating the rolls and the dessert? I hope not. Instead, rewrite the script. Visualize yourself sitting down and chatting without touching the bread basket. And when dessert comes, you order a dish of fruit. You'll be pleasantly surprised.

The next time you're in a similar situation, your actions will begin to follow your positive visualization. It's hard to believe, but try it. It works.

Third, develop positive self-discipline, making it a daily habit to rehearse every important act relentlessly, over and over again in your imagination, as if you have already mastered that act.

Fourth, set aside a few minutes of relaxation time every day to spend in guided imagery. We need to refresh and coach our subconscious with correct information so that its amazing ability to follow instructions will take over automatically and guide us to a direct hit on the target.

Repetitive self-talk over and over again is the key to winning self-discipline. A simple experiment by a behavioral psychologist in Florida highlights the truth of this. Randall Marsciana tried out a whole array of performance-enhancing strategies during a dart game.

Contestants used everything from Zen techniques to guided imagery in their attempts to hit the bull's eye. It was reported that the most effective technique was positive self-talk, which had the additional benefit of giving the players a high level of euphoria between rounds. Keep giving yourself positive feedback and coaching.

When you rehearse the correct moves and internalize them, you'll become a high-performance human being. You'll find that others will call you lucky or gifted or "in the right place at the right time." This is the typical response to those achievers who seem to have everything fall into their laps because their actions are seemingly effortless. But you'll know the secret—it's developing the habit of self-discipline that allows you to make your dreams a reality. Never lose sight of the fact that every habit is a learned behavior.

• • •

Fly Like an Eagle!

A friend of ours in Australia has a pet Osprey, which is a member of the hawk family. It was raised as a chick by a family of ducks. You ought to see it try to swim, with its talons churning the water like an outboard motor while its adopted sisters and brothers paddle smoothly with their webbed feet. The little Osprey doesn't know it's not a duck! If it is raised like a duck, it virtually becomes a duck.

Conversely, if it looks like a hawk, acts like a hawk, learns to fly like a hawk, it will become a member of the hawk family. And if you look and act like a leader, you will become a leader.

Observation, imitation, repetition, and internalization. You become that to which you are most exposed. Constantly expose yourself to successful individuals whose personal habits match their professional achievement. It's one of the most important lessons we've learned in all of our lives.

To review the steps to becoming a total winner: You use self-acceptance to discover you have all the potential you need. Self-confidence gives you the trust that you deserve to win. Self-determination puts you in the driver's seat. Self motivation puts the flame in your inner fuel. Self-expectation makes you believe in the self-fulfilling prophecy.

Self-imagination helps you dream of the future you really want. Self-direction puts that dream on paper. And self-discipline teaches you that practice makes permanent.

In the next chapter, we'll talk about positive self-projection, which is demonstrating these winning traits by the example you set.

The Power of Habit

You may know me.

I'm your constant companion.

I'm your greatest helper; I'm your heaviest burden.

I will push you onward or drag you down to failure.

I am at your command.

Half the tasks you do might as well be turned over to me. I'm able to do them quickly, and I'm able to do them the same every time if that's what you want.

I'm easily managed; all you've got to do is be firm with me.

Show me exactly how you want it done; after a few lessons I'll do it automatically.

I am the servant of all great men and women; of course, I'm the servant of the failures, as well.

I've made all the great individuals who have ever been great.

And I've made all the losers, too.

But I work with all the precision of a marvelous computer with the intelligence of a human being.

You may run me for profit, or you may run me to ruin; it makes no difference to me.

Take me. Be easy with me, and I will destroy you.

Be firm with me, and I'll put the world at your feet.

Who am I?

I'm Habit!

What Every Woman Needs to Know

Habits are replaced, not broken. It takes about a year to internalize a new, positive habit.

What Every Man Needs to Understand

A support group is a critical part of new habit formation. Take a cue from women—form a network of positive supporters, and meet or talk with them often about common goals, progress, and setbacks.

Chapter 10

———————•———————

Demonstrate by Example

This chapter is on the characteristic of self-projection. Achievers define and demonstrate by their actions who they are and what they stand for, for everyone to see. They take responsibility for who they are. They're walking, talking examples of positive self-projection.

• • •

Denis: You can always spot a successful woman when she first enters a room. Winners project an aura about them, a warm glow that shines from the inside out. They have an unmistakable presence. They have a charisma that is at the same time disarming, radiating, and magnetic. They're naturally open and friendly. They know that a smile is the universal language, the key that opens doors and melts defenses and saves a thousand words. They show others that here's a caring, sharing person.

Achievers are aware that first impressions are powerful and create lasting attitudes. They know the truth of the old saying "You never get a second chance to make a first impression."

They understand that relationships can be won or lost in the first four minutes of conversation. They've learned through experience that people project and respond according to an almost instantaneous, instinctive reaction.

Human resource professionals will tell you that many career job interviews are decided in the first few minutes of the meeting. Sales professionals know that important deals and other transactions are decided very early in the negotiation.

The simple truth is that people hire people they like. People buy from people they trust. People choose to be around people who make them feel comfortable, people who've defined themselves as being real and exemplify what they say they stand for.

To be successful, you have to know that everyone projects and receives through a different encoding and decoding system. It's as if we all work on the same computer but each of us has a private word-processing program, unreadable by any other system than our own.

Therefore, achievers realize that the best they can hope for in the communication process is a common level of understanding that will appear beneficial to the other person. There are some fundamentally consistent patterns that successful human beings follow when they practice positive self-projection. First, they always want to look their best. They know the clock is running, and they feel that since there's no time to lose, why not put your best foot forward?

• • •

Invest in the Quality of Yourself

We live in an era of electronic media where nothing is what it seems, and the news anchor's blue jeans are hidden behind the desk. All we see is the spiffy jacket and silk scarf. It's either play the game by media rules or be left on the sidelines.

Knowing the difference between internal values and superficiality is knowing the difference between quality and phoniness. The more people try to impress, the less impressive they really are. A person's self-esteem is usually inversely proportional to the stretch of the limousine he or she is riding in. In other words, that person is trying to stretch his appearance to others. If you use a limo because of convenience, no problem. But if your limo is your statement because of your conceit, you've got a problem. We've always looked at conceit and arrogance as God's gifts to shallow people.

There is a difference between quality and gaudiness and between excellence and extravagance. Women who win in life understand and appreciate the difference. For the most part, there is a direct correlation between investment in better education and materials, and the caliber of people. In that sense, you do get what you pay for in life, which is why you always seem to appreciate the achievements you've made that cost you the most dedication and effort.

This is also true with nations, as with individuals. We can't maintain our standard of living without investing in research and development of the industries and technologies that will manufacture the goods and improve the services of the future. Manufacturing high-quality goods is impossible without an educated, highly motivated, and trained work force—which, in turn, is impossible without investment.

Investment is like shopping for value more than price, buying for long-term worth, not a fleeting ability to impress. Most custom-made suits are tailored of fine materials and in classic, long-lasting styles. They also take more wear and tear because they're fitted to your body. Yes, they cost more, but they look better after 50 dry cleanings than cheaper suits after two or three pressings. Real bargains usually require real investment.

Gold is expensive because it's indestructible even after centuries on the bottom of the ocean. Diamonds are expensive because they endure. If you were buying a parachute for yourself, would you shop at a flea market?

Think of any product or service you shop for as a parachute, and be diligent about quality—consulting *Consumer*

Reports, if necessary, about failure rates and manufacturer's guarantees. If you needed a heart operation, you would, of course, seek out a qualified, respected surgeon with a record of success. Look for the same level of quality in every purchase and every area of your life. When you need expert advice, go to an experienced, highly trained person with a proven track record.

Check backgrounds; many so-called experts are charismatic salespeople with more style than substance. When buying equipment, buy the best you can afford, keeping safety, reliability and performance in mind. This includes your automobile. It will retain its value and be a bargain in the end. When developing a relationship, invest it with quality, time, energy, and creativity. Make your time with that person really count. In relationships, as with everything else in life, success requires investment.

What we yearn for most today is for leaders, friends, and associates with integrity. We are looking constantly for those items and for individuals who project the real thing. More than any other virtue we look for in people, we value honesty most. And it is in short supply.

● ● ●

Dayna: My daughter, Alissa, is as precocious as she is petite. She projects energy and self-confidence, but her brutal honesty has significantly contributed to my gray hair count!

On many occasions, her observations and confrontations have mortified me.

I'll never forget the time she was sitting in a restaurant high chair at twelve months of age observing a rather portly man being seated at the table next to us. After he was comfortably seated with his menu in hand, she leaned over and sweetly inquired, "Why is there a pumpkin growing in your tummy?" Or the time, as a three-year-old, when she bolted from my side toward a man smoking in the non-smoking section of the airport. While her index finger wildly shook with conviction, she scolded, "That's a very naughty habit, and you're going to die early."

Just recently I overheard one of her verbal volleys with a kindergarten classmate. The other child raced up to Alissa, and in a sing-song voice taunted, "My house is bigger than your house!" Alissa confidently replied, "Yeah, but you rent and we own." The child ran off not fully comprehending the insult. But later that night I heard from the child's irate father, who accused me of raising a tyrant.

There is no question Alissa's comments, though honest, were socially unacceptable. I have gone to great lengths to teach both of my children to appreciate the differences in people and to respect an individual's free choice.

Alissa carries the added burden of being an assertive female. Historically, society has not rewarded a woman who speaks her mind or defends her interests. There is still the "boys will be boys" and girls should be "sugar and spice and all things nice" mentality in our communities and schools.

Like many parents, I must help my children to strike a balance between honesty and diplomacy and temper their positive self-projection with a little more humility.

• • •

Test Your Integrity Level

Fill in each blank with a 5, 4, 3, 2 or 1, using the following scale: 5=strongly agree; 4=agree; 3=uncertain; 2=disagree; 1=strongly disagreee.

    1. I don't give in to the temptation to pad my expense accounts. _____

2. I always do as much or more than is expected of me in my work. ____

3. I never take office items—even small ones—for personal use. ____

4. If my associates were as honest as I am, our organization would never have to worry about white-collar crime. ____

5. Those who know me consider my word to be my bond. ____

6. "Loyal and faithful friend" is one way my friends would describe me. _____

7. Recognizing how readily we influence the behavior of others, I strive to set a good example in all of my endeavors. _____

8. Each day, I work at remaining honest in all interactions, both in and out of the office. _____

9. If my spouse's (or signifiant other's) emotional and physical fidelity were equal to mine, I would call myself faithful. _____

10. In general, my approach—both at home and away from home—is to treat others the way I would like to be treated. _____

Total _____

Score as follows:

    44–50 Excellent. You have winning integrity.

    37–43 Good. But there's room for improvement.

    0–36 Poor. You need to reevaluate your definition of honesty.

Project Your "Best" Self

Authentic achievers respect the fact that we usually project on the outside how we really feel about ourselves on the inside. Just as when we aren't feeling well physically we look drawn and pale, when we don't feel good about ourselves emotionally or mentally we can become lazy and apathetic about our appearance. Because this can be a detriment to our success, it is important that we apply a conscious effort to nurture and develop our "best" self. Studies show a direct correlation between "looking good" and success, so if we monitor and maintain our physical health, fitness and appearance, chances are we will experience greater fulfillment and success in life. It's never too late to get in shape, and the rewards along the way will help boost our self-confidence.

When Janet Freeman was in her 50s, she hadn't participated in any sports since high school. She took up running and has earned dozens of medals and trophies, as well as holding three track records set at the U.S. National Senior Sports Classic.

Every day this grandmother of 12, now approaching her "young" seventies, is up at 6:30 to start the morning with two hundred crunches, eighty pushups and a little stretching. After a bowl of cereal and a banana, she's off to run six miles and then swim a mile and a half before lunch. In the afternoon, she plays golf or tennis, or she line dances. She admits to resting in the evening.

What makes her run? Not the winning, just the joy of doing it—and it shows on her face. If Janet can do it, there's no excuse for the rest of us.

A well-known Helen Reddy song says: "I am strong. I am invincible. I am woman." Not long ago, we saw a woman with a T-shirt on that said, "I am woman. I am invincible. I am tired." We admit it made us chuckle, but then we began to think about the message she was projecting. How was she defining herself? Not as being capable and in charge, but perhaps as being more of a victim. Remember that we begin to project the unconscious messages we tell ourselves, and others may get the wrong impressions or perceptions about us. We must be cautious about what our clothes say about us when we're out in public. A cute sentiment on a T-shirt in a shop window can be perceived as a negative statement when we wear it to lunch.

A recent Harvard study pointed out that people who feel unattractive—or who are judged to be unattractive by their peers—tend to suffer from feelings of loneliness, rejection, and isolation.

School children who look good are actually treated better, not only by their classmates but by their teachers as well. When a friend was investigating a new school for her sixth grade daughter, the director of admissions asked bluntly "Is she slender?" Yes, she was. "Does she have any physical problems that will make her stand out from the group?" No, she didn't. "Good," said the director, "she'll have an easier time fitting in."

We were surprised when our friend told us this story, and we empathized with her annoyance and readiness to reject the school for being superficial. Upon further reflection, however, we realized that the director was just being blatantly honest and forthright. How great it would be if everyone were accepted on the basis of who they are inside, but unfortunately, that's not reality, yet. By asking if there would be any peer acceptance problems, the school was actually preparing to accommodate and intervene on the girl's behalf, if needed.

What can we learn from these insights? First, while we have no choice over the genes that we've inherited, and thus are "stuck" with our general shape, structure and skin, it's to our advantage to take care of our health and appearance and to do what we can to enhance what we've got. Like it or not, we'll be judged by the instant and lasting impression of how we present ourselves. And second, since we behave according to the way we think we look, rather than the way we actually look to others, those of us who can learn to be fairly satisfied with our physical appearance are way ahead of the game insofar as being successful and fulfilled in the game of life.

Beware the Trappings of the "False" Self

In today's cosmetic, chemical and silicone society, when we consider the true meaning of positive self-projection, there's a real need for a sense of internal value. Ideally, our feelings of success are generated from the inside first before we project them externally. Often we try to project success through our material possessions. The kind of house, car, clothing, and possessions that we show off to the world is our attempt to tell others who we are, or more likely, who we'd like to be.

The late Sam Walton, the founder of Walmart, was one of the richest men in America. Yet, he didn't feel the need to project a false self to impress others. Apparently, he drove himself to the neighborhood barber shop in a used pick-up truck and paid the bill in cash.

Linda Marcelli is the only woman to run one of the 29 Merrill-Lynch brokerage offices. Her office is the flagship in New York with annual revenues exceeding three hundred million dollars.

When she started in 1972, she had two children of her own, nine foster children, a husband, a dog, and two ferrets. More importantly she could sell stocks with the best in the business. While she was making money on Wall Street, her husband moved to Florida, where he started a highly successful tomato farm. Every week he'd drive a truckload of tomatoes to New York, with Linda working nights and weekends sorting and delivering. Did she need to show off how much she was worth? No, she knows her value, and it isn't defined by money.

• • •

Deborah: There were times in my life when I would have wanted a more impressive car, house, or clothes to show off to others. I felt self-conscious, embarrassed, and "less than" because I didn't have the quantity or quality of material possessions that certain family members or associates had. The pressures of a society that overvalues acquisition and the "finer things in life" would often gnaw at me.

Just after I was promoted to an executive management position in the Houston-based Fortune 500 company I mentioned earlier, the senior and executive level management staff spent the day in a strategic seminar off-site at a ritzy hotel in downtown Houston. As we all walked outside the lobby to give the valet attendant our tickets, the entire group was standing next to me. I nervously watched as first a black Mercedes and then a silver Jaguar pulled up, and two members of our group said their goodbyes and drove off. I prayed that I would be last, that everybody would hurry up and get their cars and drive away. But to my horror, my old 1980-something Dodge Ram pickup truck was making its way right in front of my group, the car I had taken the payments over from my sister because she didn't need a third car anymore!

Sure enough, the comments began: "Deborah, don't tell me that's your car," "Do you keep a rifle behind the seat?" "How many bales of hay can you haul in that there thing?" and so on and so forth. I knew they meant no harm by their comments, and I laughed and joked along with them. All the way home I dialogued with myself to get to the bottom of why I felt so humilated. Why would I have felt completely different had a Lexus or BMW driven up with my keys in it instead? What was this experience telling me? Why did I doubt my self-worth and self-esteem because of the kind of car I drove? I decided then and there, with my Dodge Ram pickup as my witness, that I would feel good about myself no matter what car I drove or what material possession I had or didn't have. If I decided at some point that a Mercedes would be nice to own because it is a beautiful, safe and well-crafted car, and if I could afford it, then why not? But to feel "less than" because I wasn't keeping up with the Joneses would be sheer sabotage to success. I vowed to try to be genuine and authentic in all my interactions, projecting my best self to all I come into contact with. This vow has brought me a sense of self-confidence and pride in who I am.

P.S. Men, don't get me wrong. A Dodge Ram, even a 1980's model, is a "cool" car. However, as you know, both men and women are subjected to the pressures of status, and we often look at the cars we drive as "markers" of success. Cars are usually more important to you men, having grown up with more of an interest in them, especially in the teen years. Women, on the other hand, tend to fall prey to the wearing of designer clothing and expensive jewelry as symbols of status and self-worth. It is important that we all continually look for our own value within, and then project our authentic selves to the outside world. This is the truest marker of success.

• • •

Denis: In my seminars, I tell the story of being invited to dinner at the house of a very wealthy man who lived in a huge house in an expensive development. One of the guests was a farmer, dressed in clean blue jeans, who happened to have owned the land this development was on—and who'd sold it for $200 million in cash. As the host toured people through his house, the farmer seemed more and more uncomfortable.

Finally, in the wine cellar, the host held up a bottle of red wine and announced that it was a rare Rothchild Reserve and cost twenty thousand dollars. "Great," said the farmer, "let's pop it open so everyone can have a taste." The owner was embarrassed and admitted that the wine was for show, not for drinking. The farmer smiled wryly and replied, "I thought you wanted to celebrate with us, not just impress us."

• • •

A friend's mother is in her eighties and lives alone in a large house in the Midwest. She has more than enough money to afford servants around the clock. Instead, she chooses to do all her own housework, and every morning she puts on her oldest gardening clothes and walks around her neighborhood, picking up trash that's been thrown out of cars.

One day a young man stopped her and handed her a $5 bill, thinking she was in reduced circumstances and needed the money. She tells the story with great enjoyment, horrifying her more status-conscious sisters. "We were standing in front of a church, and I told him to enter the church and put the money in the box, where it would do some good. I never felt better in my life."

More important than telling others who we are, we project by our actions the standards by which we live. But in today's Plastic Age, dominated by the flood of credit cards and the ease with which they can be obtained and used, anyone can arrange to display a Lexus or a power boat or a camper in front of the house. We can all have the latest electronic toys and the finest furnishings. But true success is having the best because it pleases you and was worth your investment, not so you can impress your friends.

True achievers may not always be able to afford to buy the top of the line or most expensive of everything, but they always do the very best with what they've got and spend only what they can afford. All it takes is a little extra effort and time in personal care and attention. Learn to follow the trends, instead of the fads.

For example, you don't need to impress others by spending a lot of money on this year's high fashion that will be out of date in three months. See how, with a little imagination and a few mornings at a resale shop, or browsing the estate sales, you can turn your home into a creative expression of your own inner worth.

Projecting your best self is one way to gain the attention and respect of people who are important to us, long enough to communicate our inside value. It's like the cover of a good book that stands out among the thousands available on the store shelf.

The Art of Communication

Here are a few tips to help you practice the art of communication.

• *Introducing yourself.* One important aspect of successfully projecting yourself is how you introduce yourself to another person. Achievers, whether in person or by telephone, lead by giving their own name first. "Hello, my name is Dayna Waitley." "Hi, I'm Deborah Waitley. What's your name?" They don't play "don't you recognize my voice?" games. In face-to-face situations, unless people are very well known to them, they announce who they are as they put out their hand. And they repeat the first name of the person to whom they are introduced, unless that person is a dignitary, in which case the last name or title is appropriate.

As simple as it may seem, by giving your own name up front, clearly and in a positive, affirmative manner, you're projecting your self-worth. It gives the other person an immediate reason to accept you as someone important to remember, and it empowers your own self-confidence.

Achievers extend their hand first. There was a time when men shook a woman's hand only if she extended it first. Today, in a world where women want equality, most men will automatically put out their hand. Women often shake hands with each other.

When anyone puts out his or her hand in friendship, shake it firmly and decisively, not with the limp-fish grip of a helpless victim. Put some authority in the handshake, but don't crush their ring finger. Firm but not hard. Look the person in the eye and communicate that you're happy to be with them.

• *Eye contact.* Along with the warm handshake, winners use direct eye contact and a warm, open smile to project interest in communication. Learn from the example set by Mary Kay Ash. Her coworkers say the roof could fall in and she wouldn't break eye contact with you.

Nothing marks self-consciousness so clearly as shifty, wandering eyes that won't look straight into our own. As they look away, it's as if they were saying, "I can't be straightforward with you because it's too uncomfortable." And nothing marks success so clearly as a relaxed smile and a face that volunteers her own name and enjoys it, while extending her hand to yours and looking directly into your eyes.

• *Active listening.* Achievers also learn the art of projecting themselves through active listening. Once the introductions are over, they fall silent. They know that listeners learn a great deal while talkers learn nothing.

It's said that's why we have two eyes, two ears, and only one mouth—so we can observe and learn more than we talk. Dr. Joyce Brothers says, "Listening, not imitation, may be the sincerest form of flattery." But always remember that listening is an activity, not a pause in your monologue.

Fran Leibowitz summed it up this way: "The opposite of talking isn't listening. The opposite of talking is waiting." How often do you catch yourself paying little attention to what the other person is telling you because you're so busy thinking up your reply? We all catch ourselves doing that.

• *Asking questions.* Achievers define themselves by asking questions when they speak. They draw the other person out. They ask for examples. They ask for feedback. They request that you say it another way, and they feed back what you tell them for clarity and understanding. They know that acknowledging your value is the highest communication skill of all.

There are dozens of books in every bookstore, filled with questions you should ask your doctor, your lawyer, your accountant, your realtor or your insurance agent. Barbara Walters has built a scintillating career asking questions and volunteering very little about herself. She conveys the impression that she really wants to know what her guest thinks. There's nothing more flattering to the human ego.

• • •

Denis: My friend and mentor, the late Earl Nightingale, one of the greatest self-development philosophers of all time, called this unique skill the "I'll make them glad they talked with me" attitude. This is a great idea that's so simple it's almost deceptive, but we have to examine it carefully to understand how it works and why.

"I'll make them glad they talked with me" can become a whole way of life. When achievers face a prospect, an adversary or a potential friend, their concern is for the other person, not for themselves.

• • •

Nonverbal Cues

When we have someone else's interest at heart, not just our own, the other person can sense it. They may not be able to describe just why they feel that way, but they do. On the other hand, people get an uneasy feeling when they talk with a person who has only her or his own interests in mind and not theirs. Many a sale has been lost because the salesperson seemed more concerned with the commission than solving the problem for the customer.

There's an excellent reason why we get these feelings about people. It's known as nonverbal communication or body language. The easiest way to explain it is "who you appear to be speaks so loudly, I can't hear what you're saying." It's a tremendously important self-projection tool when we're trying to define who we are.

We communicate by means of some 700,000 nonverbal signals. That means we have a nonverbal vocabulary that's infinitely greater than the number of words we know. That makes it easy to understand why nonverbal communication has more effect than most of us ever realize.

Whether we're aware of it or not, we telegraph our intentions and feelings. Whatever goes on in our head and heart seems to show up on the outside. What makes it difficult is that we receive most of these nonverbal communications below the conscious level of thinking. Our subconscious minds evaluate them and serve them up to us as feelings based on our past experience.

When we adopt the "I'll make them glad they talked with me" attitude, the idea of helping the other people solve their problem, we show we have the other person's interests at heart. Then the feelings they receive agree with what they hear us say, and the climate is just right for all of us to benefit. It's the double-win.

Achievers listen for the definition given by the whole person. They watch the body language carefully, realizing that folded or crossed arms sometimes means a defensive or introverted listener. They understand that hands on the hips or active gesturing can mean an aggressive attitude. Eyes can look down or away to show self-consciousness or guilt, or they can flare or pinpoint in anger or surprise.

Achievers listen to how you project yourself with extra-verbal messages. These include the tone of your voice. A frightened tremor in your speech. A nervous laugh. The unemotional monotone of the disinterested, or the rehearsed drama of the actor.

100 Percent Responsibility

People who are successful in business and personal relationships take one hundred percent of the responsibility for the communication process. In other words, they never meet you half-way or go fifty-fifty. As listeners, they take one hundred percent of the responsibility for hearing what you mean.

And as talkers, they take 100 percent of the responsibility for being certain that you understand what they are saying. They give examples, ask you for feedback, put what they say in different words, and make it easy for you to gain the true intent of their communication.

If you have trouble communicating, take a course. There are adult extension courses offered by the university in your town. Or try classes at the Learning Annex or other groups like it. Attend seminars. Join Toastmasters. Buy audio and video instruction tapes. There are all sorts of ways you can go to work on your communications skills.

Seek Common Ground

When they speak, achievers use the K.I.S.S. formula. In communications, K.I.S.S. means, "Keep It Straightforward and Simple." Project in clear, concise, simple language. Define yourself by using words and examples that don't evoke a double meaning or a hidden agenda.

Don't use vocabulary that's over the heads of your listeners. It communicates the wrong message when you make another person uncomfortable so you can feel superior.

The essence of communication is to get your thoughts across to someone else. You do that by speaking on their level, in their comfort zone.

And never forget that every word you speak has a life and a half-life beyond that. Avoid any slang expressions that will reflect badly on you. Stay far away from smutty language or ethnic slurs, no matter how funny you think they are. What's humorous to you can be painful to someone else. A casually uttered profanity will project a definition of you that isn't flattering. The poet Emily Dickinson wrote, "A word is dead when it is said, some say. I say, it just begins to live that day."

● ● ●

Denis: Finally, and most important—achievers project constructive, supportive ideas. They're neither cynical nor critical. They accept another person's viewpoint as being valid, even if it's diametrically opposed to their own beliefs. Much of the violence in the world is based upon rigid beliefs. You don't need to embrace or accept another person's belief as your own. But to live fully, happily and successfully in today's global village, you do need to make room for other people's beliefs without anger and hostility.

Demonstrate by Example

Winners say, "You know, I appreciate and understand your position. However, I may feel differently and, if so, I'd like to tell you why my position may be different from your own."

If we want to be loved, we must first project that we are lovable. Think back to the people who've had the most influence on you. You'll probably find that they were people who really cared about you—your parents, a good teacher, a close business associate, a good friend—someone who had your interests at heart.

In turn, the only people you'll influence to any great degree will be the people you care about. When you're with people you care about, their interests and not yours will be uppermost in your mind—just ask any parent.

• • •

In every area of your life, define yourself positively by paying close attention to the image you project. And make certain the image you project is consistent with your deepest core values instead of society's skin-deep styles. It's the secret of true, enduring success.

In the next chapter, we'll talk about the final characteristic of the true achiever—the diversity of self-dimension.

Poverty

Poverty is untested potential, resulting from environmental and self-imposed limitations.

Poverty is working a lifetime doing something you don't like, so you can retire and do something you like after age 65.

Poverty is having many acquaintances and not knowing any of them well.

Poverty is having so many clothes, you "haven't a thing to wear."

Poverty is eating so well you constantly have to worry about dieting.

Poverty is having every pill imaginable to cure your body's ills because you can't afford to be sick.

Poverty is being loaded with toys at birthdays and holidays and being bored silly because there's nothing to do.

Poverty is having three degrees and feeling unfulfilled in your career.

Poverty is having two cars, three TV's, two computers and a cell phone, and "roughing it" on weekends camping to "get away from it all."

Poverty is going day-to-day from one building to the next and never stopping to see the beauty in the world outside.

Poverty is spending money on make-up, deodorants, colognes and designer clothes, and still being worried about the image you are projecting.

Poverty is being a healthy, middle-class person in America, unhappy because she or he isn't wealthy.

Poverty is never being curious about the world around you and never wanting to explore it or the people in it.

Poverty is as much of the soul as it is of the body.

What Every Woman Needs to Know

You don't need to come across as more masculine to project confidence and success.

What Every Man Needs to Understand

Listening, asking questions, and understanding personal needs of others is not perceived today as being more feminine. It is the profile of the new leader-coach.

Chapter 11

---•---

Diversity in Action

In this chapter we're going to deal with the final *Psychology of Winning* characteristic shown by every successful person—self-dimension. This habit allows you to stand back and view the forest, even though you're one of the trees.

• • •

Denis: Self-dimension refers to how you project value beyond yourself in everyday living. You are most successful when you can give yourself away to others, unconditionally, without expecting a payoff. The catch is that you can't give away what you don't feel for yourself. You know that unless you love yourself, others won't love you. It's also true that you can't respect and love others unless you respect and love yourself. You can need people, or you can use them, but there can be no mutual respect without your active practice of positive self-dimension.

The healthy high-achievers function effectively because they maintain a healthy dialogue between themselves and others, treating everyone with the same respect, integrity, and care as they accord themselves. True self-dimension is understanding that diversity embraces not only the things we can see, such as gender, skin color, ethnicity, age and other physical traits; it also includes the most important diversity of all: the diversity in our beliefs and in the way we express our emotional intelligence.

Achievers look beyond themselves to find the real meaning in their lives. They put it all together as the rarest of human beings—a complete and total person. They have the ability to step back from the canvas of their lives the way an artist steps back from the canvas to gain perspective. And they make their lives a work of art, their individual master-piece that illustrates the big picture.

When you have the habit of self-dimension, you can take the *Psychology of Winning* information that you've experienced in this book and move it off the shelf and out into the universe. The greatest example of self-dimension a winner can display is that quality of earning the love and respect of other human beings.

• • •

The Fruits of Sharing Success

Mother Teresa, the founder of the Missionaries of Charity in Calcutta, India, and winner of the 1979 Nobel Peace Prize, exemplified one of the most visible examples of positive self-dimension. Her mother always taught her, "When you do good, do it unobtrusively, as if you were toss-ing a pebble into the sea."

By the time she was 12, she wanted to become a nun, and she entered the Loreto order while still in her teens. She was trained as a teacher, spoke several languages, and taught European and Hindu girls in a convent school for many years before leaving her order. She wanted to help the poor rather than teach the children of the privileged. Despite bureaucratic, financial and health challenges, her work has continued uninterrupted around the world. In her last years, she concentrated on the children affected by the AIDS epidemic that is rampant in India, and also children abandoned by their parents. Working to age 90, she maintained her sense of humor while finding ways to overcome tremendous obstacles. Her laughter was reflected back from all the children she helped. Her legacy will outlive her for centuries to come.

Mother Teresa always handed out a card to anyone who asked for it, a card that was printed for her by one of her benefactors. It says, "The fruit of silence is prayer. The fruit of prayer is faith. The fruit of faith is love. The fruit of love is service. The fruit of service is peace." Here's a woman who took the time to step back and look at the big picture—and spread her message across the world.

The real meaning of the *Psychology of Winning* isn't standing victoriously over a fallen enemy. Self-dimension is extending a strong hand to one who's reaching, groping or just trying to hang on. It's helping your opponent to her feet. Achievers know that there'll be no lasting peace on earth until there's a piece of bread in every mouth and milk for every child. Achievers create other successes without exploiting them. They plant shade trees under which they know they'll never sit. They know that true achievement in life happens when caring and sharing people help even one other individual to live a better life. As Eleanor Roosevelt said, "When you cease to make a contribution, you begin to die."

The "Inner Circle" Journal Exercise

Not all of us can be a Mother Teresa or an Eleanor Roosevelt. For most of us, self-dimension begins with the inner circle, our family. Jot these questions in your journal, leaving room for the answers.

Is your family a winning team that works, plays, worries and rejoices together as a unit? Or is it a place of strife and discord that the kids can hardly wait to escape from as soon as they're old enough?

Are your personal relationships precious to you? Do you reach out to friends and family members on a regular basis, no matter how busy you are? Or have you lost touch except for birthdays, anniversaries, reunions, and a duplicated form letter tucked into a holiday card?

Do you take the time to be proactive and find out what's causing your husband or significant other to lose sleep at night or to be in a bad mood at dinner? Or do you react to his negativity by taking it personally and adding to his burden?

If you're successful at living, you get it together with your loved ones, with your friends and with your community.

High achievers may love their careers, but they're not married to them. Still, they care about their company and its product, its fairness to its employees, and its honesty in everyday dealings.

They vote and stay current with what is happening in their cities, states, and nation because it's their duty and right as citizens. They answer the summons to jury duty because it's one way of paying back what they've been given. They support the government, whether or not it's the one they voted for, and work within the system to correct wrongs as they see them.

Achievers live a well-rounded life. They put emphasis on every area of their lives. Are you a financial success with plenty of money to spend but no time for children? It's said that on one's deathbed, no one ever worries about not spending enough time at the office. Happy, well-adjusted children come from homes where they have unconditional love and attention, not conditional money and toys. Give your children roots and wings, instead of loot and things. Roots of self-esteem and wings of self-determination, so they can fly from the nest and contribute to society.

Losers try to buy love and trust, and they fail every time. Do you spend all your time earning money to support your family, but not enough time caring for them? Do you have a highly paid position so you'll take care of company business— and a highly paid governess to take care of your children? Do you have a winning soccer or volleyball team as an outside activity, but a losing, neglected family inside your home?

Are you attractive externally, and shallow and egotistical internally? Do you pay more attention to how things look than how people feel? Do you take from life what you want, even if it deprives someone else?

Losers change the Golden Rule to read, "Do it to others before they do it to you." They have the "I win and you lose" attitude. The sphere that represents their lives has all the pressure at one point. When that sphere bursts, the fallout will be more dramatic than any bomb.

The "Double-Win" of Stewardship

Real achievers practice the double-win attitude of "If I help you win, then I win—and when I win, you win, too."

The double-win in society and business is called stewardship. There's a new emphasis in corporate America on customer service, team building, honesty, and trust. The most profitable, successful organizations in the world have mission and vision statements that workers, regardless of their pay scales, can relate to their own job descriptions.

You may be surprised to learn that in the midst of downsizing, outsourcing, and reengineering, there is a tidal wave movement toward performance pay, incentive pay, employee profit sharing, day care and wellness services offered by the company, and a general trend toward companies becoming more like "extended families" to their employees.

In the 21st century new world, which is already here, everything is changing. In fact, change is the only constant. And adaptability is the only security.

The Adaptable Attitude in Action

The following five suggestions will help you put an adaptable attitude into action:

1. Instead of fearing change, expect it. View change as normal. Constantly check yourself for how flexible you are to new ideas, surprises, and other situations that demand adaptability to change.

2. Use the salvage-the-situation approach. When things don't work out just the way you planned, don't panic or go into a blue funk. No matter what game you're playing, one loss doesn't make a season.

3. Ignore the little disappointments and irritations in order to reach your larger goal. Many people let the little things get to them and ruin their performance, attitude, and chances for success. Adaptable people learn to live with a certain amount of inconvenience, embarrassment, discourgagement, and antagonism. They concentrate on what really counts—the major goal or objective.

4. Develop your innovation techniques. When faced with constant change and insecurity, innovation is vital. Read biographies of the new innovators and entrepreneurs. You may be surprised to find that many of them simply put a new twist to an old idea.

5. Remember the prayer of Reinhold Niebuhr: Change what you can, accept what you cannot change, and ask for the wisdom to know the difference.

In the old world, leaders were warriors. Today, leaders are facilitators. Yesterday, leaders demanded respect. Today, leaders encourage self-respect. Yesterday, leaders command-ed and controlled. Today, leaders empower and coach.

• • •

Wisdom of the Feminine

Dayna: One of my favorite books is China's most popular book of wisdom, written in the fifth century B.C. It is ironic that this ancient wisdom could be so laser-focused on the leadership qualities we need as we enter the 21st century A.D. In the Tao Te Ching, the Yin is the feminine aspect of lead-ership, and the Yang is the masculine side.

In practice, the leader must express more of the Yin and become more of a healer, in an open, receptive, and nour-ishing state. The Yin is illustrated as being like water, and the Yang like rock. Water, at first glance, seems to be less strong than rock. Water is fluid, soft, and yielding; yet water will wear away rock, which is rigid and cannot yield.

The wise leader knows that yielding overcomes resis-tance, and gentleness melts defenses. Just as it was in ancient Chinese wisdom of centuries past, real power comes from empowering others.

• • •

We have given lip service to this statement throughout the 20th century, yet few leaders and executives have prac-ticed this trait. Those who have, have prepared the soil for growth and harvest in the future. Those who try to lead from the old, intimidating power base, with the military command and control model of leadership, are obsolete.

In recent years there has been a rash of firings of CEO's of many of our largest companies. Reasons most cited for the abrupt dismissals include abrasive personalities, autocratic management styles, lack of vision and flexibility, lack of people skills, and out of touch with customers and employees.

Successful CEO's of our best-run companies believe that the more power leaders have, the less they should use. Power, in the new world, multiplies only when it is shared.

That's why we believe women are ideally poised for new positions and roles of leadership in business, government, education and the professions. Women constitute more than 50 percent of the workforce. More women own and are starting small businesses than men. The greatest movement in the world today is toward home-based businesses, where relationships are more important than positions, and where work spaces have replaced work places. Networking has always been part of a woman's world, and it was a man, Bill Gates, founder of Microsoft and the wealthiest man in America, who observed, prophetically, that in a networked world, we can ignore geographic boundaries to do all our shopping. It will be like one great big beauty and hair salon, where everything will be bought based on word-of-mouth on the Internet.

As we enter the 21st century, there will be more women entering the highly educated, highly skilled professions than men. The average age of individuals in the workforce will increase to 45 in the next decade. Given today's immigration and birthrates, one in every four Americans will be Hispanic, African-American, Asian, or Middle Eastern. Less than 30 years from now, these minorities together will become the majority, and European Americans will become just one more segment of a thoroughly integrated nation.

So the young, adult, white male can look forward to a new status as a minority, working quite likely, sometime in his career, under the supervision of a woman. Without a doubt, all of us will be living in a multicultural environment offering a positive, rich, personal growth experience. It would be wise for all of us to unhook any lingering prejudices we may have today, lest we feel the effects of it going full-circle and coming back at us.

Yin and Yang Synergy

As the glass ceiling continues to crack and is, we hope, shattered in the business, professional, and political arenas of society, women and men need to develop positive self-dimension and enter into a partnership of understanding in their respective points of view, so they can work side-by-side with equal opportunities for achievement and fulfillment.

Whether men agree or not, women do, generally, listen more openly and fully than men. Women are more naturally intuitive. They ask more questions and draw the other person out. They facilitate a group better, which is imperative in today's team-oriented marketplace, because they more readily subordinate their egos for the good of the group. Women are better at customer-focus needs.

They are naturally better communicators because their communication skills mature earlier than do males'. The fact that there are more men in power in the communication arts is strictly a result of the good-old-boy network that has been in place for several centuries.

Because men have been raised to believe that the world is theirs to conquer, they tend to view risk as normal and desirable. Because women, in the past, have served in the role of keeping the peace and teaching the young, women have learned to seek security as normal and desirable.

Generalizing to make a point, men need to listen and nurture others more. Women need to assert and risk more. And both sexes need to view these qualities as neither masculine nor feminine. Just healthy Yin and Yang synergy.

In our own research, we have come across some disturbing trends related to women's liberation and assertiveness. Along with new freedoms, women have been emulating some of the most destructive habits promoted by a formerly male-dominated society. Lung cancer in women, which 20 years ago was minuscule, is on a vertical curve straight up to become a leading cause of death in women. Heart disease, formerly a man's domain, is also on the rise in women. There are more Type A women now, reacting to stress rather than adapting to it.

Women drink more, smoke more, swear more, swagger more, and fight more, as if these behaviors gave them a rite of passage into the male-oriented competitive arena.

The image of Bubba, with a cigar or a pinch of chewing snuff between his cheek and gum, belly-up-to-the-bar, tossing down Margaritas or brewed ale, spewing forth profanities, is hardly the kind of multicultural role model we need for healthy women or men.

In defense of women who are emulating the wrong heroes, we need to point out that men still control most of the big advertising budgets that layer our lifestyle habits from cobwebs to cables, and they are more responsible for this subliminal seduction than women themselves.

Male Habits that Women Should Forsake

1. Cigarette smoking—Thanks to Sir Walter Raleigh and his followers, women now have equal opportunity for lung cancer and cardiovascular disease.

2. Cigar smoking—When you kiss someone who's been smoking a cigar, it's like licking an ashtray!

3. Tobacco chewing—Put a little pinch between your cheek and gum, and the next thing you know, the women's softball team has mouth cancer like real major leaguers.

4. Swearing—There's nothing more masculine than rolling the "f" word out of those ruby red lips.

5. Swaggering—If male professional athletes can do it, why not everyone?

6. Swilling—Being a two-fisted binge drinker is the ultimate rite of passage into a formerly male world.

7. Tattooing—If it's the mark of a he-man sailor or biker, it must be good for the liberated woman.

8. Road rage—If men can use their cars as weapons, why not women?

9. Intimidating—Making people fear you is a cover-up for low self-esteem.

10. Violence—So far, women have not fully embraced this male method of problem solving.

In a *Fortune* magazine interview some time ago, several top women were interviewed on how they were managing in these chaotic times. Rebecca McDonald, who at the time was president of Tenneco's natural gas subsidiary and the youngest woman senior executive in the industry, said that today management is a blank page, now that hierarchies are obsolete. She said, "You hear a lot of talk about changing the way we teach little girls because they're taught to listen and accommodate, while little boys are taught to win at all costs. I wonder if, really, we shouldn't rethink the way we're teaching boys. The rigidity that comes with expecting to win at all costs doesn't necessarily play to the new skill sets needed in the global marketplace.

"Those management skills include dealing with needs, issues, and market forces that are not clearly defined." She goes on to say that "Women have a higher tolerance for ambiguity because they've always been responsible for attending to the emotional needs of others, which are very fluid. Women learn to read between the lines and come up with creative solutions for accommodating people." She's not suggesting a touchy-feely approach at all. Results are still the bottom line. She's saying that women are especially suited to today's demands: listening, communicating, and getting to the root of the problem. It's what women have trained for throughout history.

Another top woman executive, Willow Shire, was also on the cover of *Fortune* magazine, and she commented that "Women are used to juggling four or five things all the time. A history of disenfranchisement helps, too. We were never invested in the old boy club," she says, "so when it's time to tear down the old system, we have nothing to lose."

Women have a destiny as world leaders in government, business, the arts, the professions, education, and the family. This is the best time in history to be a woman, alive and reaching up. It is also a time for balance, perspective, and self-dimension.

True Wealth

Positive self-dimension means spiritual dimension, your relationship with your Creator, and being in harmony with the divine order that shapes the entire universe. It means seeing the perfection and the beauty in nature and recognizing the imperfection in our attempt to reshape it to a form we think would suit our lifestyle better.

The *Psychology of Winning* can help you achieve both inner and outer wealth. We're grateful to live in a society based on free-market competition, where we can own property, start a business, do our own thing and prosper. We believe we should have the right to earn as much as we're willing to work for, by providing products and services that benefit as many people as we can. The key is to work, create, and provide for the benefit of others, not to exploit them, cater to their fears, play on their insecurities, titillate their sensual perversions, or feed their obsessions.

In your quest to win, provide a service that improves the quality of others' lives and the environment. Develop and market products that you would gladly share with your own children and grandchildren. You will reap a harvest that is both tangible and intangible. Both are good. Having money is one important aspect of wealth—but only one.

To the sick person, wealth is health. To the lonely person, wealth is someone to talk to and share life with. To the estranged person, wealth is hearing words of love and forgiveness.

Some people with the Midas touch are impoverished in spirit and in happiness. Some people who can just barely put food on the table are filled with joy.

Real poverty lies in cruelty and abuse of others, dishonesty, insensitivity, gluttony, laziness, anger, self-criticism, and guilt. Just as important as gathering the rewards associated with our goals is eliminating the impoverishing thoughts and behaviors that rob our lives of resources and destroy inner character.

• • •

Denis: My dear friend and colleague, Dr. Hans Selye, has been called the pioneer and father of stress research. Dr. Selye told us that self-dimension can be accomplished only by making a constant effort to earn the respect and gratitude of our business associates, family members, community friends, and neighbors. He suggested that rather than attempt to accumulate money or power, we should attempt to accumulate goodwill. This is possible only when we do things that will help others succeed. Hoard goodwill, Dr. Selye advised, and your home will be a storehouse of happiness. "Anyone can attract the curiosity and the attention of crowds," he believed, "but the blessing is to earn the trust and respect of one child."

On your way to success, make plans to:
- Grow friendships, not just bank accounts
- Grow diverse associations, not just diversified investment portfolios
- Grow relationships with those you want to spend time with when you retire, not just a retirement account
- Grow loving bonds with your family, not just bonds from which to clip coupons

Time Is of the Essence

Most important, with their positive self-dimension, winners have a keen awareness of the value of time, and they know that once they have spent it, it's gone from their lives forever.

Time never rests, never looks forward or backward. Life's raw material spends itself now, this moment, which is why how you spend your time is far more important than all the material possessions you may own or positions you may attain. You can renew your supply of many things, but like good health, that other most precious resource, time spent is gone forever.

When we were five years old, one year represented twenty percent of our total lives. At 50, a year represents two percent, or one-fiftieth, of our life experience. No wonder it took so long for holidays to arrive when we were in grammar school, and little wonder also that after age 50, when a year represents such a small portion of the time we've already spent, it goes by in a seeming blink of an eye. Like a video cassette speeding up as it rewinds, accelerating wildly near the end of the reel, so goes your remaining time as it dwindles down.

Each yesterday and all of them together are beyond your control. Literally all the money in the world can't undo or redo a single act you performed. You cannot erase a single word you said, nor can you add an "I love you," "I'm sorry" or "I forgive you"—not even a "thank you" that you forgot to say.

There are no sadder words in the language than "I meant to". "I meant to call"; "I meant to say I love you"; "I meant to give you one more hug"; "I meant to say I'm sorry." We all have an "I meant to" story. We all know that a moment missed is a moment lost forever.

That's why achievers develop a deep respect for the value of time. They don't waste time the way losers do—chasing it, squandering it, or trying to hide from it under a mask of cosmetics. They understand the mortality of their own bodies, and they mature and adapt to age gracefully and positively.

• • •

In her classic tale *West with the Night*, Beryl Markham wrote: "Never turn back and never believe that an hour you remember is a better hour because it is dead. Passed years seem safe ones, vanquished ones, while the future lives in a cloud, formidable from a distance. The cloud clears as you enter it."

And opera star Leontyne Price said: "You should always know when you're shifting gears in life. You should leave your era—it should never leave you."

They knew that growing old is a state of mind and that spending time is inevitable. That's why the achievers in life treat their bodies as if they were meant to last forever.

Etty Hillesum was a Jewish woman who was born and raised in the Netherlands. Her diaries reflect her life, which ended in 1943 when she was only 29 years old. She wrote, "Before, I always lived in anticipation—that it was all a preparation for something else, something 'greater,' more 'genuine.' But that feeling has dropped away from me completely. I live here-and-now, this minute, this day, to the full, and this life is worth living."

The singer Pearl Bailey said, "Sometimes I would almost rather have people take away years of my life than take away a moment."

•   •   •

Deborah: How short and therefore incredibly precious our time on earth is, a series of moments lived and experienced, then gone forever. Time is of the essence, and the essence of life can be enriched by how we spend our time. Life becomes more bittersweet as we grow older and realize that, like most cherished commodities, the value of time significantly increases as the supply becomes limited. And oh, how we wasted precious time in our youth! We can start now, however, to capture and savor our moments.

Every so often I experience what I call "death flashes." They seem to arrive out of nowhere, whether I'm driving on the freeway, falling asleep at night, or gazing out my window. The frequency of their occurrence seems to be increasing with age. An intense feeling of a strange, almost sickening anxiety jolts my mental, physical, and emotional senses. Along with it comes the realization that at some point in time I am no longer going to be here. I am going to die. Everyone I know and love is eventually going to die. It is a sobering realization. Yet instead of allowing this overwhelming sensation to be a negative experience giving rise to anxiety, fear, and depression, I welcome the insight and arousal it stirs up inside me. I am suddenly awakened from the "slumber" of my everyday routine, and life takes on new meaning and intensity.

I am allowing the dimension of this experience to enter my life, and I am making a conscious effort to savor the moments of time, especially when I am spending them with my loved ones. Realizing that life can change ever so quickly without a moment's notice, I spend as much quality time with my parents as possible and see my remaining grandparents every chance I get. I stay in close touch with my siblings and intimate friends. Even when my teenage son and I have our "heated discussions" and arguments, I try to remember that someday I will look back on this precious time and wish I could relive it.

Developing a self-dimension that is more mindful of the present has greatly enhanced the quality of my life. As I embrace all the success and fulfillment present in each moment, time seems to stand still, yet expand all at once—perhaps a glimpse of heaven.

• • •

Enhancing Your Dimensions of Time

If you're a winner, you live fully in the present while expecting something even better in the future. You know that life is what happens while you're making other plans. You understand that the best laid plans are often written in the sand at the tide line and will be washed away and changed time and again. As the novelist Faith Baldwin put it, "Time is a dressmaker, specializing in alterations."

You take the time to watch the rosebuds open and listen to what others have to say, finding value in all inputs. You take time for your children, knowing that too soon they'll be gone from home. As the prima ballerina Gelsey Kirkland put it, "Fortunately for children, the uncertainties of the present always give way to the enchanted possibilities of the future." It's up to you to open that future to them with your guidance and enthusiasm.

You take time to play the way you did as a child, because when you lose that childhood enthusiasm, you'll begin to grow old.

You take time for old people, knowing that the old people live for the hope of communication and attention from their loved ones. You know the truth of Emily Dickinson's statement: "We turn not older with years, but newer every day."

You know that age is nothing but a number, and you welcome it as a new challenge. Rose Kennedy, who was over 100 when she died, remarked, "I'm like old wine. They don't bring me out very often, but I'm well preserved." Actress Glenda Jackson commented, "I look forward to growing old and wise and audacious." And author Alice Walker summed it up neatly when she wrote, "It must become the right of every person to die of old age. And if we secure this right for ourselves, we can, coincidentally, assure it for the planet."

If you're an achiever, you take time to relish your work, knowing that scaling the mountain is what makes the view from the top so exhilarating. However, you also know that you must retain control of the hours you spend. Golda Meir said, "I must govern the clock, not be governed by it."

You take time to read, knowing that books are the fountain of wisdom. They take you places you may never visit in person. They add dimension to your existence. The American journalist Agnes Meyer admonished, "Time is the one thing with which all women should be miserly."

You also take time for nature, knowing it's to be enjoyed and protected. Eleanor Roosevelt reminded us, "Perhaps nature is our best assurance of immortality." And you take time to promote your own health because you know that health is your passport to the future. It's a gift that you don't recognize or appreciate until you've lost it or thrown it away.

And most of all, you take time to love. To love another is to look for the good, to encourage and allow that person plenty of growing room to be all that she or he could ever be.

Katherine Hepburn said, "Love has nothing to do with what you are expecting to get—only with what you are expecting to give—which is everything."

Achievers don't live in the past. They use it as a classroom, learning from it, enjoying their successes and their memories, but they know that change is inevitable. And they don't live in the future either. They know that the future may never come.

The true achiever lives in the present moment. She knows that the only second of time over which she has any control is this instant—and it's a heartbeat away from being history.

For each of us, the clock is running, but there's still time to win. First, step back from the canvas of your life and gain perspective, like an artist constantly shading a painting that's being improved on every day. Look at yourself as a total person.

Ask yourself: "How do I fit into my family? My company? My community? The nation? The world? Creation?" Consider the ecological cycle, the double-win—if I help you win, I win. If nature wins, we all win.

There's a woman in Garden Grove, California, who understands how to be an achiever. Mardi Reynolds is a retired nurse, so crippled with chronic pain that she spends part of her life in a wheelchair. Although she lives alone on $614 a month in welfare payments, and suffers from lupus, osteoporosis and rheumatism, since 1986 Mardi has been distributing bread and other baked goods to the poor and needy in her hometown.

Every Tuesday and Friday, she collects loaves of bread and pastries from the local supermarkets. She loads them in her car and hands them out. On Sundays, she cooks and feeds the homeless in the park. Mardi Reynolds says she's carrying on a tradition. When she was totally broke, she saw an older couple handing out food.

She says, "I started going there for meals. I was so grateful, I vowed when I got back on my feet, I would repay their generosity by helping others." As we learned earlier, what goes around comes around. What are you doing to help feed your community?

Self-Dimension Grid

On this grid are 24 different items. As you read each item, ask yourself "How true is this of me?" For example, taking the first item, "Have a variety of close friends," is this 10 percent true of you, 20, 30, 60, 80 or 100 percent true of you?

Statement   How True of Me? (10 to 100)

Have a variety of close friends.   _____

Spend time alone thinking,
meditating, or praying often.   _____

Exercise vigorously each day.   _____

Have adequate time spent with family.   _____

Have a job that pays me well.   _____

Am already engaged in the career I want.   _____

Am involved in community activities.   _____

Enjoy reading nonfiction books.   _____

Make friends easily.   _____

Statement | How True of Me? (10 to 100)

Statement	How True of Me? (10 to 100)
Have studied religious or spiritual teachings	_____
Eat nutritious, well-balanced meals.	_____
Regularly write or call members of the family.	_____
Am creating an adequate retirement fund.	_____
See opportunities for advancement in career.	_____
Belong to local association(s).	_____
Enjoy educational TV programs.	_____
Enjoy meeting new people and going to parties or group events.	_____
Attend church, synagogue, religious services, or engage in spiritual practices.	_____
Am involved in sports regularly.	_____
Enjoy family reunions/gatherings.	_____
Have a substantial savings account.	_____
Am really good at and enjoy my work.	_____
Have volunteered for a community project.	_____
Like to go to museums, fairs, libraries to see what's new.	_____

Now transfer your scores for each of the 24 items to the following grid. Add the numbers in each of the eight columns and total them.

SOCIAL	SPIRITUAL	PHYSICAL	FAMILY
1. _____	2. _____	3. _____	4. _____
9. _____	10. _____	11. _____	12. _____
17. _____	18. _____	19. _____	20. _____
TOTAL	TOTAL	TOTAL	TOTAL

FINANCIAL	PROFESSIONAL	COMMUNITY SUPPORT	MENTAL
5. _____	6. _____	7. _____	8. _____
13. _____	14. _____	15. _____	16. _____
21. _____	22. _____	23. _____	24. _____
TOTAL	TOTAL	TOTAL	TOTAL

Now turn to the Wheel of Fortune and plot the total points for each of the eight areas of your life on the line below the title of the area. When you have plotted all eight points, connect them to get dimension or perspective on the shape and size of your own wheel. How round is your wheel? How will it roll down the road of life? Which areas of your life would you like to spend more time developing?

Chapter

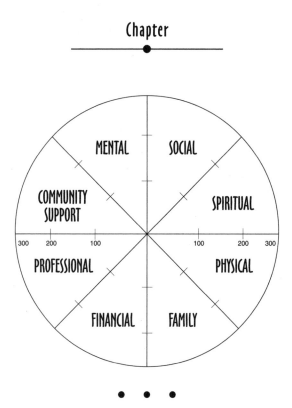

• • •

Denis: Learn how to grow out of yourself and into the world of others. Plant a shade tree under which you know you'll never sit. Set some goals that may benefit your children, the children in an orphanage, the employees of your company, future generations, or your own city 50 years from now.

And remember that true positive self-dimension is living well for yourself, so that you can give yourself away to benefit others.

You've discovered the 10 characteristics of high achievers and how you can use them in your life. In the final chapter, we'll focus on that elusive butterfly called happiness and how to seize the best that life presents—and do it now!

• • •

What Every Woman Needs to Know

Part of diversity is understanding the many roles you can take upon yourself, without losing yourself.

What Every Man Needs to Understand

An open house at school, a child's piano recital or an important lunch with a loved one is as important as a Board of Directors' meeting. When they ask you why you are missing the meeting, tell them it's an IRS conference. (They don't need to know that IRS means Intimate Relations Schedule!)

Chapter 12

•

Delight in Living

In this final chapter we'll review the traits of winning women and show you how to take delight in what you do, making happiness a journey, not a destination. More important, you'll discover that what you do is not as important as it is that you do something—and don't wait another minute.

• • •

Denis: You've learned the 10 characteristics of a total winner as I first researched them for the original *Psychology of Winning*. And you've had them updated and tailored to give you habits that can be learned and used to live a successful and fulfilled life.

First, you discover your potential through self-acceptance, just as you are, a work of art in progress. Next, you deserve to win by gaining trust and self-esteem. You decide to excel because you are self-determined. You are ignited by the inner fire of desire from within, or self-motivation, and dare to believe in your dreams through self-expectation. You dream your reality because of your creative self-imagination. You design your future with self-direction and specific goals. And you dedicate your mind with relentless practice and self-discipline.

You demonstrate by example your core values by self-projection, and you are diversity in action as a total woman with self-dimension.

• • •

Besides these giant leaps, there are little secrets that ensure total success. In this final chapter, we'll talk about these secrets and show you how you can build a life of happiness, self-actualization, and fulfillment starting right now!

10 Secrets of Success

The 10 secrets of total success that we write about in this chapter have been touched on throughout the book, but where overlap occurs, it's because the ideas are so timeless and work so well.

1. There's no point in becoming an achiever if you don't find joy in the process. All truly successful people, no matter how much sadness they have to contend with, have an inner wellspring of contentment. They still find pleasure in giving to others, no matter how little they have themselves. Helen Keller said, "I am only one. But still I am one. I cannot do everything, but still I can do something; I will not refuse to do the something I can do."

But while you're giving to others, don't forget to give to yourself. Happiness is a journey, not a destination. Lillian Watson said, "Happiness is not in having or being—it is in the doing." If you work so hard at achieving that you never stop and put your life in perspective, your victory will be a hollow one.

Anne Frank, from a well of wisdom far deeper than her years, left us this message: "We all live with the objective of being happy; our lives are all different and yet the same." In other words, whether you're hiding from the Nazis in a cramped attic or trying to get your boss to notice your contributions to the marketing plan, your need to be happy is a constant. Happiness is a habit, not a result of achievement.

Part of being happy is projecting happiness. Opera singer Beverly Sills makes this distinction: "A happy woman is one who has no cares at all; a cheerful woman is one who has cares but doesn't let them get her down."

Beverly Sills, who was gifted with one of the most beautiful voices of our time, was blessed with two children. One is autistic and the other is deaf. Both have never been able to appreciate their mother's talent. Despite this, Beverly Sills has been called "Bubbles" by her friends because of her quick laugh and cheerful disposition.

A wise person said, "Pain is inevitable, but misery is optional." No one gets out of this life without at least a taste of tragedy, grief, catastrophe and challenge, but how we deal with them says more about who we are than all the testimonials we can gather.

Katherine Hepburn put it this way: "Life can be wildly tragic at times, and I've had my share. But whatever happens to you, you have to keep a slightly comic attitude. In the final analysis, you can't forget to laugh."

So the first secret of success is to keep your sense of humor and make happiness a goal you achieve every day.

2. Give more in service than you expect to receive in payment. We've heard people say the reason they want to start their own business is so they won't have to work so hard. Can you imagine? There is no harder taskmaster than yourself.

Giving more in service than you expect to receive in payment may sound outrageous to some, but it is the secret of every self-made millionaire. We all live in a time-starved world, so we don't necessarily need to work longer hours. We do need to do the things the rest of the population are not willing to consider.

Too often we miss the great opportunities because we don't want to demean ourselves by doing jobs we feel are beneath us. The account executive isn't about to go back to typing her letters, even though her secretary has the flu and the temp won't be there until tomorrow. So she frets and gripes and causes a scene when she could have done the work herself without a problem.

Helen Gurley Brown tells about Laura Willi, who works as an assistant in a nursing home handling bedpans, changing sheets, and tending to the other needs of the elderly residents. It's not glamorous work. It's not even very pleasant most of the time. But Laura says, "I walk approximately three miles a day from my apartment—those cross-town blocks are long. I go there whether its raining or snowing. Those old people need me." Laura Willi is in her nineties. The job's not too tough for her.

Here are some action ideas:

- Do every project as if you were self-employed and your retention by each client depended upon how well you did it.
- Take rejection as a temporary inconvenience and persist. Margaret Mitchell, who wrote *Gone With the Wind*, submitted her manuscript to over 80 publishers and was rejected by all 80 before the 81st published it.
- Think of yourself as a newly arrived immigrant in this country. What effort would you take to become successful?
- Take the time to follow through on the smallest details. Remember, it's the littlest things that cause the biggest problems. Carry this motto with you daily: "Elephants don't bite, but fleas do!"

3. Develop a sense of "nowness." Don't lament or long for the past. Stop worrying about or living in the future.

As we mentioned early in the book, the past is history. The future is a mystery. Today is your gift. That's why it is called "the present." Stop, take a deep breath and enjoy the day. It's time to lift some of the stress off your shoulders and allow yourself time to savor what you've earned.

In your journal write this word—"No!" This is to remind yourself that you don't have to be a Superdaughter, a Supermom, a Superwife, a Superemployee, a Superfriend, or a Supervolunteer. It's time to say "Yes" to you and "No" to everyone else. Just the other day we heard about a woman who went on strike. Her husband and children weren't keeping their part of the bargain, and the house was a mess every evening when she came home from work. "Okay," she said, "if you won't do it with me, do it without me." It didn't take long before there was chaos in the house. The laundry wasn't done, the cleaning never happened, groceries were never bought, and the dog was never fed. Shortly thereafter her family realized what a treasure they had sitting on the front lawn with her lemonade in one hand and her "On Strike" sign in the other.

The father and the kids got it together and soon everything was sparkling clean, the refrigerator was full, the dog was walked, the laundry folded—and only then did they humbly invite Mom to come home again. Now, *you* learn to say "no", "enough," and "this time's for me."

And then simplify your life. Make an inventory both of the material clutter that takes up space and is never used and of the clutter on your schedule, the nonproductive activities that create stress without adding to your enjoyment of life.

Again in your journal, answer this question: "In addition to the duties I must perform, what do I really want to be spending my time on?" And then *do it*.

4. Life is a self-fulfilling prophecy. What you see for yourself is what you'll get. If you're cynical and depressed all the time, your life will be played out in shades of gray instead of the colors of the rainbow. If you get to feeling sorry for yourself, stop by a children's hospital or a senior citizen's retirement home, a burn unit, or an orphanage. Then try to feel sorry for you.

Surround yourself with laughter and you'll bring it with you wherever you go. Country singer Dolly Parton says, "The way I see it, if you want a rainbow, you have to put up with the rain." If it's raining in your life, think of the flowers that will follow. We've found it best to surround ourselves with optimists, which isn't hard in our family.

In your journal, write these two words: *Mastermind Network*. A mastermind network is the coordination of knowledge, in a spirit of harmony, between two or more people for the attainment of a definite purpose. To be successful, join a group of achievers who are success-oriented. Meet once a week in the morning or after work to discuss similar goals. Mastermind networks are powerful.

When the people around you think positive thoughts and give you positive feedback, you begin to think the same way.

Instead of greeting the new day by saying, "Oh God, it's morning," you'll be filled with enthusiasm: "Good morning, God!" The inflection you put on your life will affect the outcome of everything you say and do.

5. A touch is worth a thousand words. One of the telephone companies used the phrase "Reach out and touch someone" to sell its service. Try it—reach out and touch someone with the positive ways you are learning here.

● ● ●

Denis: My mother, Irene, who was celebrating her 90th birthday when this book was published, wrote a touching poem about the time my sister, brother, and I grew up and went our own ways. It speaks to the idea that a touch is worth a thousand words.

Where Are My Children?

Have you seen anywhere, a dear boy and a girl, and their small winsome brother of four?

It was only today, that barefoot and brown, they played by my kitchen door;

It was only today, or maybe a year, it couldn't be twenty, I know,

That laughing and singing they called me to play, but I was too busy to go. Too busy with my work and my life to play, and now they've grown up and they've wandered away.

Someday, I know, they must stop and look back, and wish they were children again. And, Oh, just to hold them and hug them again, I'd run out my kitchen door.

For there's never a chore, that could keep me away, could I just hear my children call me to play.

Where are my children? I've got time—today!

●　●　●

6. *Clear focus always precedes success.* Focus is the most obvious and most overlooked reason for success or failure in the world. The mind only acts upon specific data. If you put a nebulous instruction in your desktop computer or PC, it cannot open the program you want.

Most people never do sit down and write out what they want to accomplish. I know one woman who refuses to even think about what she wants because she doesn't want to be disappointed. As Alice said to the Cheshire Cat, "Which way ought I to go from here?" And the cat replied, "That depends a good deal on where you want to get to." "I don't much care," says Alice. "Then it doesn't matter which way you go," says the cat, his grin getting bigger all the time.

Most Americans reach retirement age without any financial security except for what they hope the government will hand them every month.

Among professionals, such as doctors and lawyers, only five percent are saving adequately for retirement. You can't blame this on the government or the economy. It's a simple matter of not setting a goal and focusing on attaining it.

You remember we said that when you set a goal, it must be specific and it must have a deadline. We all want to have our senior years well-funded, but when our goal is "to have enough money when I retire," there's no chance we'll start saving and investing in our twenties—or thirties or forties, for that matter. The goal is too indefinite and too far off.

Setting goals can be especially daunting for women because we have so much on our plates. Even though women pay sixty-one percent of the family bills and write eighty percent of all checks written, we forget to put some money aside for ourselves. We know we should pay ourselves before we pay anyone else, but there is always a more pressing bill that needs attention.

Treat your future like a utility bill or mortgage payment. Make your "life mortgage" payment the first bill you pay each month. Set an amount, get a payment book, and put the same amount each month in a mutual fund or money market account. Think to yourself, "If I don't make this payment, my future will be disconnected, and my pride as a senior citizen will be repossessed by having to be a ward of the state or my family."

Like Scarlett on the steps of Tara in *Gone With the Wind*, we figure "Tomorrow is another day." And when tomorrow finally comes, we're surprised it got here so quickly and we're so unprepared.

Go over the goals you've written in your journal. If you haven't made them specific enough, do it now. Set a timeline for accomplishing them with long-term, medium-term, and short-term deadlines. Read over your goals every day and check off the ones you've attained. You might even get a little package of gold stars from the stationery store and give yourself a pat on the page. There's no more important secret of success than setting goals and making yourself attain them.

7. *Your literacy and vocabulary define you better than a fingerprint, and your lack of education brands you with a scarlet "F."* We live in the Knowledge Era, where information access is instantaneous and global. Knowledge is the greatest power, and lack of it is the greatest enslaver. Consider the shelf life of your formal education to be about 18 months, which means you must dedicate yourself to being a lifelong learner and continue your education on your own time.

The unabridged dictionary has about 500,000 words, give or take a few thousand, and 80 percent of the time the average adult uses only 400 to 800 of them. The word we use most often is "I." While mega-bookstores are proliferating, less than 10 percent of us will buy or read a book in the next 12 months. And many of the people who do buy books never read them. They feel it's enough just to pay for them and let them sit on the coffee table.

A woman in Chicago makes a very respectable six-figure income as a salesperson for a manufacturer. She dresses well, looks great, owns her own house and has money in the bank. Externally, she's got it together. She's hip and likable and has scores of friends. But she doesn't have a college degree, and that makes her feel insecure. She worries about whether she's using the right word or if a sentence is grammatically correct. No one would know unless she told them, but it eats at her and keeps her from going into new situations where she's afraid she'll embarrass herself.

Don't allow yourself to get into this same situation. Buy a vocabulary book or an outstanding audio program. You can learn a few new words every day. Keep a notebook and a dictionary near your reading chair. When you come across a new word, look it up and write it down.

We have a friend who does the *New York Times* Sunday crossword puzzle in ink! Her vocabulary is off the charts, but her notebook is always open, and there are dictionaries all over the house. She doesn't use all those words when she talks to people, but she knows them, and from that knowledge comes a visible self-confidence. The added benefit is that her children outscored their classmates on the SAT vocabulary tests. It's an interesting fact that vocabulary scores are usually consistent with success in college and with financial success later in life. What our children see is what our children do.

Do you have a library card? Do family members have one, too? A library card is still the best bargain in America. Everything that's taught in universities is available on the library shelves, ready to be opened and read. Make it a regular family outing to spend an hour at the library and open up new avenues of learning.

Don't overlook the correspondence courses, continuing education classes, seminars, and home-study courses. You don't need a degree to get a college education. Distance learning via online university extensions and the Internet is available everywhere. Increase your computer literacy with e-mail, web browsers, fax dispersal, Internet telephone, foreign language software, and your own home page on the Web. The truth is, those individuals who are not online soon will be in some kind of breadline in the future.

●

8. *What we get out of life is in direct relation to what we give.* It's a restatement of the old law of cause and effect and the scriptural reference to sowing and reaping.

The giving we're talking about is on multiple levels: we give to charity, we give to family and friends, we give to employers, and we give to the community.

But if you barricade yourself and your talents and never give what you can sell, you'll be a poorer person—and a lonelier one.

An Arabian proverb says: "If you have much, give of your wealth. If you have little, give of your heart." And the actress Eleonora Duse said, "When we grow old, there can be only one regret—not to have given enough of ourselves."

If you have no money, you can volunteer your time. There's no one on the face of this earth who can't do something to bring a smile to another person's face.

If you have no time, you can send a check. No amount is too small now that government subsidies have been cut back. When you watch your local public television station, do you get annoyed by the incessant fund drives? We all do, but they need to bring in cash so the programming can continue. Instead of complaining, call in your pledge. If you have no money, figure out a way to raise some. Have your local merchants keep change jars on their counters and collect the coins for the cause.

If there's anything we want you to take away from this book it's this—*if it's to be, it's up to me.* Never say, "Never." Always say, "I can."

9. *Our subconscious mind can't tell the difference between what's real and what's imagined.* When you allow yourself the freedom to be alone and talk to yourself in positive, strengthening affirmations, you enhance the creativity that unleashes your potential. Fantasize about successes you've not yet had.

A writer we know thinks about her book being published. She sees herself signing the contract, receiving the advance check, and opening the package with the advance copy. When she walks into a bookstore, she imagines her name on the placard announcing this month's book signings. She plans what she will write during autograph parties and works on the guest list for the party she'll have at publication.

How often do you allow yourself to fantasize? Do you encourage yourself with self-talk? Do your serve as your own personal cheerleader or your own worst critic? Do you expect to achieve your goals and plan how to enjoy them?

Get to know the creative side of you. Ride your bike, fly a kite, smell a rose, walk in the woods, have a picnic in the park. Spend time with *you*, allowing your imagination to soar.

And laugh with yourself. As Katherine Mansfield wrote, "When we begin to take our failures nonseriously, it means we are ceasing to be afraid of them. It is of immense importance to learn to laugh at ourselves."

10. We must set free that which we most want to possess. Love is an expression of the value we place on a person independent of his or her ability to meet our needs. Authentic love makes you want to set your partner free, not possess him or her. Therefore, you must feel love inside yourself before you can give love away.

To risk being loved or rejected, you must first feel worthy and lovable enough to overcome insecurity. This is what it all hinges on—self-esteem. Actress Shirley MacLaine wrote, "The most profound relationship we'll ever have is the one with ourselves." When you love yourself, you treat yourself with the respect you deserve: You nourish your body, your mind, and your soul. Until you think of yourself as lovable, there's no way that you can think of yourself as equal.

Actress Marlo Thomas made a very important point when she said, "One of the things about equality is not just that you be treated equally to a man, but that you treat yourself equally to the way you treat a man."

Do you love yourself just as you are, or do you find reasons to dislike yourself so you can excuse your failures? Do you feel guilty if you're selfish with your time? Think of some examples and tell yourself that you are your biggest creditor. You need to pay yourself on time, just as you pay your other bills.

Are you confident about your abilities without being vain? Are you happy being you? If you were to eavesdrop on the women you admire most today, you would never trade places with them because your own blessings may outnumber theirs and their tragedies may overshadow their perceived triumphs.

The message here is to know yourself and love yourself. Gloria Vanderbilt grew up with everything money could buy and little else. She wrote, "One of the goals of life is to try and be in touch with one's most personal themes—the values, ideas, styles, colors that are the touchstones of one's own individual life, its real texture and substance."

● ● ●

Deborah: We have given you a lot of information in this book: ideas, stories, examples, action steps, key points, and exercises to help you live the best life possible. As you've read these chapters, you've been assimilating the insights and are already incorporating them into your life. We've just described ten secrets of success which, when followed, greatly improve your life. I want to share one final secret with you that has worked wonders for me in all the avenues, highways, toll roads, and alleys of my life's journey. How about creating your own secret of success, one that is entirely unique to you? It can be your own personal motto or success creed to live by each day and remind you of your significant place and contribution in the grand scheme of life. You may choose to use an inspirational or meaningful quote from someone you admire, or develop your own statement describing what success means to you, or how you want to live, or a certain value or philosophy, whatever suits your delight. Because that's what it's all about, isn't it—joy, happiness, and fulfillment in living. That is truly winning.

My personal motto happens to be by my side and in my consciousness at all times, throughout the pages of my journal, in my daytimer, on my walls at home, on my desk, in my car, and in my very being. I heard it from a former business associate of mine, Lawton Llewellyn. My personal secret of success is:

"Plan your life as if you were going to live forever—and live your life as if you were going to die tomorrow." So go out there and live—as the glorious woman you were meant to be—forever "winning" at being you!

● ● ●

Dayna: To delight in living, you must have a forgiving attitude toward yourself and other people. We live in an imperfect world where problems are normal indications of change in progress. Remember that for every one thing that goes wrong in your day, there are at least 50 that go right.

A recent event has taught me to keep my sense of humor about the inevitable mishaps of daily life. One of my friends from college was surprised recently at the grand opening of her new branch office. As a bank manager, she organized the entire event, but her husband surprised her by sending a magnificent floral arrangement to the festivities.

The flowers arrived with a large banner that stunned many of the guests. The inscription on the banner read: "Rest in Peace."

My friend's husband was embarrassed, upset, and agitated. He felt that the wreath had ruined the whole event. He promptly called up the florist and read her the Riot Act. After offering her sincerest apology, the florist concluded the conversation with one last thought, "Look at it this way, sir," she said. "Somewhere a man was buried today under a wreath that said, 'Good Luck in your new location!'"

Keep your sense of humor! Laughter is the best medicine. Delight in living by accepting yourself and others as changing, growing, imperfect human beings.

• • •

21 Reasons Why the 21st Century Begins the Millennium of the Woman

1. Women are starting companies at twice the rate of men. The number of female-owned businesses in North America has grown to over 8.5 million. Women-owned companies employ one out of every four workers and generate more than $2.5 trillion in revenues.

2. Women take education more seriously. In North America, about 90 percent of women complete high school, compared with 86 percent of men; 30 percent get college degrees versus 26 percent of men. And this trend is accelerating.

3. Women develop verbal skills more rapidly than men. This advantage is important at the dawning of the knowledge revolution.

4. Women try to resolve conflict peacefully. If there ever was a critical trait for solving problems in a global village, this is it. Since we all live in a "borderless" world of instant communication, the ability to gain consensus among differing interests is paramount to our survival.

5. Women are waiting much longer to get married because that is only one of their major life goals. Education, service, career development, and self-actualization also are important goals.

6. Women can and will be elected President. A University of Chicago survey reports that nine out of ten voters would vote for a qualified woman to lead the country.

7. Women are no longer spectators in athletic competition. Thanks to Title IX—the federal mandate that opened the school door to equal-opportunity sports many years ago—the results are finally showing. Nearly three million high school girls participate in sports, up 50 percent from a decade ago.

8. Women are more conscious of their health, not just their looks. The $50 billion dollar nutrition and fitness industries are driven primarily by women. Although women have a longer life expectancy than men, women also want quality of life to go with the quantity.

9. Women have become breadwinners. Women are the main income producers in one out of four two-income households.

10. Women have better networking skills. The 21st century heralds a workplace based more on relationship power than position power. Being a team player and team leader is more important than being a charismatic superstar.

11. Women have better listening skills. Through centuries of playing a supporting role, they have fine-tuned the ability to listen for the root of a problem by asking questions.

12. Women can adapt more readily to change. The new management skills include dealing with less than clearly defined needs, issues, and market forces. Because women have always been responsible for attending to the emotional needs of others, which are very fluid, they learn to read between the lines and come up with creative solutions for accommodating people.

13. Women can sublimate their egos. In simpler times, the egotistical boss could survive. Now leaders must empower others. If you don't have the discipline to do that, or if you have an ego that has to be stroked all the time, you're not going to build an effective team. Failed automaker John DeLorean specified arrogance and ego as the causes of his downfall. He said he could not bear to have the car with his name on it go down in defeat.

14. Women are more intuitive. While men tend to look at the bottom line numbers, women look at the whole person. Women have a keen awareness for being able to spot a phony better than most men. In an "infomercial world" loaded with fads and promises, it's important to be able to go to the "gut" when assessing a business or personal relationship.

15. Women understand customer service. Women, more often than men, make the decision on which home to buy. They consider functionality, practicality, resale, location, convenience, and safety. Men consider how it looks overall and how much it costs.

16. Women can let go of prejudice more easily. Since men are more territorial, they protect their turf and their own kind more vigorously and are suspicious of outsiders.

17. Women readily delegate authority. The most important determinant of job satisfaction is work autonomy. People now value the chance to make their own decisions and influence what happens on the job even more than the amount of their pay. Women don't need to take the credit for success as much as men do.

18. *Women encourage experimentation and tolerate mistakes.* In the world's best-managed companies, employees are rarely criticized for mistakes. Employee suggestions are truly wanted, and management understands that people will not speak up in an atmosphere of anxiety or fear.

19. *Women are better at reinforcing positive behavior.* Since women have the major role in early child development, they have come to understand that good behavior needs reinforcing, while bad behavior needs correcting to the targeted behavior.

20. *Women understand how important it is to be there in person.* No e-mail, phone call, card, or expensive gift will ever replace the value placed by taking the time to be there in person for a person you care about. Open houses at school, recitals, rehearsals, conferences, and performances mean a thousand times more to the child when the significant adult role model shows up. As we become adults, this need never diminishes. Being there in person shows how much you really care.

21. *Women are geared to surprises!* More than anything else, the new century will be full of surprises. Downsizing, outsourcing, electronic commerce, sudden fashion and market shifts, new consumer tastes, and constant change. Although women may have been security-seekers more than risk-takers in the past, they have had to study more, work more, give more, overcome more, and tolerate more than men have in pursuing their dreams. The ability to tolerate uncertainty and to hold things together has been a hallmark of their development. Patience and persistence are virtues that will bring women to the forefront of global leadership in a millennium filled with surprises.

Plan for suprises. Expect them. Accept them. Know yourself. Love yourself. Share yourself. And all the rest falls into place naturally.

The 21st century will mark the greatest positive transformation for women into positions of leadership in every aspect of society.

The great coloratura, Joan Sutherland, had it right: "You can listen to what everybody says, but the fact remains that you've got to get out there and do the thing yourself."

So now you've read it. Now just *do it—with delight!*

About the Authors

Denis Waitley is one of the most sought-after keynote speakers in the nation on self-leadership and change management. His audio and video programs are used as basic training tools by individuals and companies worldwide, including corporate executives, government officials, educators, athletes, families, and students of all ages. He is the author of four New York Times bestsellers: *Seeds of Greatness, The Psychology of Winning, The Winner's Edge,* and *Being the Best.*

Dayna Waitley is one of the fastest rising stars on the national speaking circuit, and a consultant to major corporations on personal and professional productivity. She was recently nominated for the international Speakers Hall of Fame (along with Barbara Walters and Diane Sawyer).

Deborah Waitley, President of Individual Excellence, Inc., is a highly regarded management consultant to major corporations on change management, process improvement, leadership, and quality. She holds a master's degree in counseling psychology and a doctorate in psychology from Union College graduate school.